How Small Brides Survive
in Extreme Cold

How Small Brides Survive
in Extreme Cold

poems
by

Steve Shavel

Acknowledgments

This book could not have come together without the help of Polina
Dimova, Teresa Grow, Miriana Ilieva, Shannon Ketch, Ed O'Connell,
Lori Shine and Matthew Zapruder.

The poem "Unh." was chosen by Heather McHugh to appear in the anthology
Sad Little Breathings & Other Acts of Ventriloquism (Publishing Online)

Library of Congress Cataloging-in-Publication Data

Shavel, Steve, 1961-
  How small brides survive in extreme cold / Steve Shavel.-- 1st ed.
      p. cm.
  ISBN 0-9723487-3-5 (alk. paper)
  I. Title.
  PS3619.H3574H69 2003
  811.6--dc21

                              2003006166

Book designed and composed by J. Johnson
Text and Display set in Sabon
Cover Art by Ariel Kotker

Printed in Canada

9 8 7 6 5 4 3 2 1

First Edition

Contents

For my parents LaVerne and Marc
and my brother Ross

Fit the First

Vimalakirti

What is the time beyond measure
when we are always in the same place?

I am pissing, lavishly,
into an ox's hoofprint,
never ceasing.
All day
the iridescent flies
wind around the lime tree
graze my reverie.
Silkworms
strip the mulberry
of her raiment
devouring, devouring.
A gentle frass
rains down.

If I were a bluefly, say,
or an angel
I'd rush into your ear
and so be heard.

Instead I find
I'm rooted to the spot
to this one — how to
put it — unconfutable
way of life.

Every instant a "lion"
seizes on a hide
the color of a gazelle slipping away.
That very instant
the lion perishes
foundering into its own fury
— the inarticulate core of roar —
and trailing a white mane of oblivion.

Every instant
through fist-sized bundles of fiber optics
a million words disperse,
meant and unmeant, or strewn
like loosed beads.

Meantime here am I
attempting the "unconfutable,"
threading what might seem to be
an extreme path between two middles:

one, relentlessly half-assed —
the yet-unspent
radio isotope
loitering before eternity —
the other,
half-assedly relentless
rooted to non-abiding,
the way a wave mauls the shore.
Nevertheless here I remain
just pissing in the abyss,
nothing left to say
and still saying it nevertheless.

Why this must be
the genius of ingenuousness!
Such indeed

is the "incomprehensible" example
of the bodhisattva Vimalakirti
couched in the discourse
of a willed illness, suffering
the birthlessness of all things —

dissembler, disabuser,
expounder of a thundering
silence, the well
within the well —

hierophant, prestidigitator!
who might palm an entire sederunt —
arhants and bodhisattvas both,
reclining on lion-thrones yet —
or fit Mount Sumeru into a mustard
seed.

Somewhere,
at the very limen
of awareness, semis
are pounding down a highway
sounding as if they
really had somewhere
to get to.

You slink by and I
eye you and you eye
me and I wish I were
made out of stone. So
still I dumbfounder there
like some stupid marble cupid, with
        the billion-world galaxies
streaming down,
and the hoofprint,
        never filled!

Unh.

Distant sliver chrysler building
see the sequined lice ascending

(A mote in somebody else's sky?
or maybe a beam in your own)

I confess, I once nursed a secret love
of architecture — worse yet,
I once loved a secret nurse of architecture —
her starch elixir!

A tendered lozenge
a fluctuating spoon —
"stupendous"
in the opinion of pundits —
a cough, a kiss
"each one molded
with a unique residue
of the curvilinear
vocation . . ."
Such, no less, their plaudits.
So high did I aspire.
O holy corbels!
O spire —
of zippers!

High on a rooftop in Alphabet City
loosing over-ripe melons over the parapet
and looking down
          on how circumspectly
the Abecedarians make their way,

'like a sickbed'
'like a sockethead'
'a suspension bed'
'on a ziggurat.'

And so it went night after night
and so passed an entire epilogue —

'Lob me a cantaloupe,
if it not displease thee'
and 'Prenez les fruits crepuscule.'
'Come again?'
'Those avoirdupois of green amaze I mean.'
'Sure thing.'

Nights in white cotton
and gauze badinage
          loose muslin
          of the flue's effluvia
in the land of Nod east of Eden
staying up
          until skyscraperfall,
until the first corpuscular glimmerings of dawn . . .

East river
          volgaboatmen
                    intoning the old
                              garbagebargedirges —

we laughed and laughed
an entire epilepsy,
a sprawling two-fisted epicenter.
Hemingway by way of Bayreuth.

High on a rooftop in Alphabet City —
well not a city exactly,
more of a Freak and Malignant Crystal —
poised over numbstruck and chronic youth: piss-
mired poets,
somnambulist artistes
feigning insomnia,
poised over the whole chambered necropolis of it
a fist   a socket   a hive
dense and boiling with light:

O vertiginous burgeoning
O dutiful
O psychopomp,
by what kabbalizing
by what tumescence
what ferment of torment
of the primordial alphabet soup
has it come to this?

We laughed and laughed
an entire episode,
down in the land of Odd
just east of Even —
while uptown a whole metropolis
rocks in grand mal seizure
          and topples
götterdämmerungenlich.

And I'm so very patient
I'm so very patient and
one final honeydew to go
when she confides,
'By wingèd words only
you'll win me or lose me.'
'Then
administer the scimitar
if it not thus far displease thee.'

Hacking it open we stand back in amaze
dumbstruck —
encountering strong moonlight.

Crenellation chimney pots
with ventilation crowns revolving
like Himalayan prayer wheels . . .

High on a rooftop in Alphabet City
she and I only, and —
why, it's Padmasambhava
          clad only
in the seven ornaments of bone!

(The prognosis of yogis was unanimous,
e.g., Bear,
'These bones are not
disposed in an entirely
unstartling manner!')

Unh huh. Words were beyond us now
and so were platitudes. Connecting up
the gematria of the streets, that is plenty.
the plaint of a sirene is plenty —
the one that bores through my tympanum

while the two of us strike
significant attitudes. This one means
cattle-in-full-lope, and that. . .
Why, it's the Statue of Puberty!

We laughed and laughed
an entire epitaph.
I left my limp
beside her golden door.

Five Churches in Barcelona

(Sant Pau del Camp)
A stained and amniotic light
leaking through the slits
of bevelled ashlar fit with alabaster
slivered to the lambency of dream
and set about the apses' undulant sweep
like epicycles of a lapsed astronomy:
and as it eclipsed one time the womb's samadhi,
kicking against the pricks of inwardness,
and discovered to the soul, that anchoress,
by aperture her captivation to the body,
immured as it were within the skull's autonomy —
the grave of image and wake of every sleep —
so now with all the speed of like, the sleight of seem,
the fastness of that than which there is no faster —
has broke this bastion romanesque to bits
and left a shell of self bereft of sight.

.   .   .   .   .

Her asides and slant approaches,
        Stella Maris
        Maria Stellans.
Her vacant arcades, occasional
vocables
reiterant of prayer-mutter
echoing off walls, columns
unencumbered of much of the usual
baroque-barnacle encrustation
ever since the anarchists torched the place
in the Civil War (it burned for eleven days,
a scorched keystone overhead to attest) —
all backdrop now
to the finest magic lantern show bar none
in the Barri Gotic,
the blurred hues touching on
some fine point of forgotten doctrine.

Half-past nones
and across a no-man's-land of flags,
stones
one time worn smooth by faith,
God's sad search beacon concludes
its slow diurnal sweep,
now only dustmotes stray incense
caught in its tinting.

Stella Maris
Mare Stellarum.

Standing in the *Santa Maria del Mar*
Christianity continues not making sense
miraculously.

.   .   .   .   .

Most of the saints are gone from their nooks and jambs
beside the portal
          folding into its own stone.
To find them you've got to look inside.
Somewhere in there in the gloom
of the cavernous *Maria del Pi*
is room enough for each and even,
beneath the floating vulva of heaven,
a neglected sinner or two.

.   .   .   .   .

Still open to the elements
and already a ruin
ensconced in its cranes and scaffolding,
it sits and sulks, Pleistocene reliquary,
caress of carapace, an obsolescence.

No longer by the mineral hoarding
of the stalactites and stalagmites it
so palpably takes after,
nor by the natural logarithm
of a nautiloid — the angels'

spiral staircase of scale,
and electrons' macroscope —
not by the trajectory
of actual flowering, fructifying
and decay on the branch,
legumen or drupe,
puffball and amanita —

sadly,
not by any of its recent accretions
in any sense of the word
unfolding,
the *Sagrada Familia* sits and broods
on a flagrant betrayal
          and gaudy disregard
of entropy's design:
the anti-Tintern Abbey.

.   .   .   .   .

From this perspective,
a stone's throw maybe two from the *Catedral,*
only a steeple shows over the barbican
forming one side of the courtyard
of the Museu Frederic Mares.
Picture, if you will, the spire,
typical of its genre,
knobbed and crocketted
filigreed and studded
          with a bestiary of spouts
and hemmed in on all sides
by a stand of its own young.

More and more intricate the pattern is drawn
up to the tip, as many angles
as can dance on the head of a pinnacle —
and there
fastened to the apex
under an immaculate sky,
a canopy of blue
right out of Fra Angelico,

a monumental cast surveys the city,
Santa Helena I'm told, her garments
ripening in verdigris.
One hand steadies with a cross,
simulacrum of the True One
I suppose,
the other extended in a sort of
"Noli me tangere,
I can do it myself,"
or more like *1' aleta,*
the salute the boy gives
after clambering to the top of those human towers
always going up around here
come some feast day or other.

She's the latest and presumably last
of six centuries' cumulus,
after the cupola and after
the Viollet-le-Duc-like facelift
(inaptly flamboyant). Her feat
is the crown of an architectonic,
but also
       a giddy-
             making
     circus
        stunt
like the ta-da! of a clever universe
just before collapsing
from the malady of its own weight.

But the spectacle continues.
Five gulls
     in slow interlocking sweeps
derive all the theorems of Euclid.
Before long she's bringing to mind
St. Francis offering a morsel
by reason of the number of birds converging:
for in late afternoon it seems
all the gulls of Barcelona
sick of the port and parking lots
search out this unlikeliest of roosts.

Picture it if you can:
one for every finial, crocket and spout,
they preen against the scenic backdrop
like tourists posing for a picture
or squabble over vantage —
and Santa Helena perched amongst
whited with their stucco

wheeling as ever across
sidereal space, haze, smog,
iridian archivolts,
or streaming through the bright curls of cirrus —

and as ever, toppling over
with unparalleled equanimity,
her serenity matched only by the sun's
tripping along its ecliptic . . .

Picture a jet that cuts across this picture.
It trails a vapor of script like an annunciation.

Imagine the steeple in storm now.
It's a sudden, garrulous storm,
like the onset of a subway,
like the inrushing of an angel
where a crowd of fools fears to tread.
Imagine the gargoyles
          in their proper element.
They look the very picture of garrulousness.
Practically gushing at the mouth . . .

Relampagos, relampagos
each approaching discharge
torn from its own howl
the way effect flees in terror of its cause.
Picture moreover Sta. Helena in the midst
like a masthead tossed and straining for port.
Her cross (St. Elmo's now it seems)
trained in the general direction of the absolute
is beginning to pick up signals,
ions racing around in the general excitement

glowing, reconfiguring:
Picture a lone prospector
in an Etruscan silver mine —
Look — there!
you just missed it.
She's touched the seam.

The Analects of Lady Mondegreen (1)

"They hae slain the Earl a' Murray
And laid him on the green"

I.

The night was hung inside its black sheathe

The scallion, at first tinged with moondrink

There is a strong chance
      of a hundred winds

The early phase of life is vast

The key to time
      will fit the lock

He crawled with care around the larch

This plank was made for walking on

Tame the sheep with the dark wanderers

It is a dense crowd in two distant ways

The serpent matches the scroll

To have is better than to wait and vote

The clan gathered on each dull night

The child whipped sated us

II.

It is late morning on the old wallflower

Yellow and fat the curtain slides back

A joy to every child is the swan boat

The petals fall with the least proof

(Thunder over Jericho)

III.

Writings of small fish cluttered the nets
Code is used when secrets are sent
(Jerk the cord and out tumbles the gold:)

Taste and cleanse the most dirty brass
Pluck the bright bruise without weeds
Wipe the sparrow from the front of your red shirt
Slug the mails with requests of this book
Stop whistling and watch the boys march

IV.

A thing of small note can cause despair
She was waving on my front lawn
The grass stains stretched into the distance
Even a just cause makes a woman strong

She was kind to sick old people
He flogged the old mill with a crooked stick
A force equal to that would move the earth
That guy is a writer of a few banned books

Shake the dust from your shoes stranger
Let's all join in to sing the last chorus:

Thunder over Jericho
Travels may stain your hands green
Thunder over Jericho
We waltz with one step in evolution

Yo-Yo Ma

Whoever it was first contrived
a whinnying caterwaul
from the unlikely cross product
of horsehair and catgut
never I'll wager foresaw
these careening scales these
notes like dust motes in a slant
of sun, legatos
like gnats
        slinging
about a common and raddling
        vortex, nor yet I'll bet
the consequence in this
precipice of sound, the number-
scarped cadence at whose profound
my ears, my sorry ears
buffeted by double-stops
auto-obbligatos
the cantering counterpoint
        the concatenation
an elision of ideas like vowels in heat
grow long and furred and
pointed as, well, consciousness itself,
itself on some accounts
a 40-or-so hertz resonance
shuddering down the length of all its axons.

The cello is a chasm hollowed.
A sarabande labors over the bridge.
It is bowed with the weight of the whole world on it.
The pines groan, a pain so round
you might well call it
an orotundity. And loss
is the rosin shed there,
a redolence of camphor
and far Lebanon,
residues of benjamin
and aromatic gums,

the mead-hall's ruined timbers
the cavern's travertine,
perdition's oakum and pitch.
The sarabande says my love
lives somewhere over on the other side —
then steps off the catwalk

and out on the high wire
      where now
by the guttering light
      jade and faded vermilion
of certain chinese lanterns strung there
      we can just make out
grimalkin and a palfrey
      caparisoned in rich brocade
capering a stately gavotte,
      much bowing and scraping
mummery and flummery
      as of an antic bergomask
in a christmastime pantomime.
      And then the limber tripping gigue.

We've all heard the analogies enough
to architecture and mathematics — the
timeless forms bestowed somehow on time
as from on high,
the celestial proportions of the spheres
puissantly grinding out
a feeble polyphony over the number-
scape of some Pythagorean sublime. It's
the same ideal resurgent
in all those fashionable pat reductions
ranking the performance
as epiphenomenon
of the composition. (Recall Schoenberg's notion
of a consummate musical evening's fare:
alone, hunched over the score, perusing.)

But here now taking place
is something else as well,
something unforeseen,

a tenebrious, sonorous,
altogether chthonian sort of thing,
the way the passing subway
temblors through the girders and into
your joints, a welling up
from deepest recesses of the race —
a maze-dance in broad Knossos:
a spell-compassed barrow heaped
over a low retreating hall, its
slumbering rank of merovingian kings,
mice nesting in parchments, snakes
coiled in the fallen crowns:
a subterranean race of teutonic dwarves
with un-disneyish names like Alaric,
Chilblains and Havoc
toiling in the forges, and the symbol-
laden torques they fashion there:
the millennia-long vigil of a terra cotta army
for an emperor who with the rest
of his dynasty is long since
returned to clay. (But notice
his empire still stands.)

And where these vectors intersect
a cello stands akimbo on a stage,
and there wrestles a man with it
deep into the night.
Sometimes so artless is his
articulation he seems to vanish
into the fantoccini
manipulating as from above the strings
on which these our actors have supervened
an elision of forms like conjugate beasts
harpy, manticore, camelopard.
Sometimes with labored breath
he reappears astride the contrivance
so we can feel the strain of every fingering
even of the sinew which shrank
and so by sheer exertion bodies forth
the illusion of parts — Jacob *and*
the angel.

Then again the bolt of his attack
as from an escarpment of cloud,
a reckless trajectory, like
pissing off the platform
nearer and nearer my God unto thee
training your arc on that third rail . . .

Suddenly I'm understanding String Theory,
by which all the world all phenomena
are seen to be the squirming after-effects
of those vermiculate superstrings
vibrating in hyperspace like a Bach
solo cello suite
                    unspooled
                              in the suspense
                                        of a falling third
then spun back up again
and around the world
in a heedless
          headlong gallopade
towards a promised resolution.

And finally that long-awaited usurper-king
the Theory of Everything
limps on stage to announce
that he cannot accept the birthright
of his hairy brother
the Theory of Nothing, and
that one cannot rule without the other,
the Waxing and the Waning Year,
Science and Conscience, etc.,
and that even music has its sulking
precedent and twin,
proceeding as it does
as all things cadent
from the fury
of a black and retractile
silence.

Martha Stewart

Simply flip a poem over and, voilà!
a sturdy soapbox
to stand on. Perfect for those days when you
just *have* to pontificate. Now

very carefully
turn it inside out — see?
There's an old man and his cello
adrift midway between two atoms.
Just the medicine
for that occasional "mope." Now:
fold it into a fedora
and guess what — you've got yourself
a dandy hat to wear.
A hat that doubles as a philippic!

Next I'll show you how to turn
that tainted Baudelaire of yours into a
thousand origami steeples. But first:
open the door and see all the peepholes.

The Analects of Lady Mondegreen (2)

I.
Speedy men can beat this trap of mine
(Race makes up for lack of painting)
"We are the men who work the middle of the road"
These thistles the just claim

The room is crowded with a wild thought
"Bail the bed to stop it from sinking!"
The little tales they are false
A strong bed may scare your partner stiff

The Lieutenant waved when the wind blew
The pirates seized the crew of the lost ship
They floated on the raft to summon the white bats
Salt becomes fond with time

A shadow of dirt fell from the vampires
He made a skill of wrinkled actresses
The fish twisted and turned on the bent hook
This is the rainy season for creeps

II.
The vamp of the shoe had a gold buckle
The gall deepened in the eyes of the sweet girl
Dreamboat heroine
These girls do less good than others

Find the twin who stole the chrome necklace
Soak the cloth and drown the sharp needle
Draw the chart with heavy black vines
Shipmarks are different from coastal plains

Take shelter this time and keep still
The theft of the pearl penny is kept secret

III.

The third act was dull and tired the players
He carved a fate from the marble block
At the column he put the sun to his ear
The hilt of the sword was pondered with fine discernment

The blouse of midland turned to waste
The cramp is no small danger to the swimmer
Takes a big trout to catch a worm
What joy there is in reading!

IV.

The abrupt start does not win the prize
Press the heather with your metal feet
Tremble the spark and thus the flames will spread
The urge to write short stories is rare

The large palace had hot water taps
The storm walls were lined with colored flowers
There the floodmark was ten inches
Pages bound in cloth make a book

The Etruscans used to give costly gifts
The ripe plum is fit for a king's crown
Guests evolve
The snail is never one

Heed the white mouse and flower scents
The mad pope was on the dry carpet
He picked up the palace for a second gold
The prince ordered his fig chopped off

V.

Five years he lived with a shaggy dog
It took wild things to frighten him
The dogface is both rare and costly

VI.

Sweet dreams
Eat plums fairly plump
Mind the trout before you go out
Say it slowly but make it ring clear

A Kabbalist's Guide to the Kitchen

The day is short, the task is great...the reward is abundant, and the master is urgent.

With pitiless and stainless steel, the horn-handled
to be adorned with a row of white knuckles.

[A]nd behold,
there was a place on the hinder part westward.

Pirke Avot 2:20

Ezekiel 46:19

What I most admire in a woman is her incisors.

You must pass between the clean and the unclean.

You will cleave between the sea and its foam. You must geld the honey from its comb.

You will pass between the knife and its smile.

Listen in . . . it is the sound of canines grinding down a nightmare.
The scrape of keel on a foreign shore.

It is KETER the crown, a razor cutting its own edge.

But who can recount for me the dream the seraph dreams coiled at tongue's root?

Wrathful decrees of the Procurator Pediculus Humanus Capitus

A hecatomb forgotten *sha'atnez tsemer U-fishtim: satan-'az metsar U-tofism.* Vide Abraham Azulai, *Hesed le-Abraham*
Sulzbach 1685, II, 27.

Mirrorwise, lest you be snatched backwards up the stovepipe

What do I know of the left and of the right, of the creation or the chariot, the thirty-two paths of Wisdom, the Fifty Gates of Understanding, or the Two Hundred and Thirty-one Ciphers of the alphabet?

Eli, Eli, Lomo asavtoni. In fier und flahmmen uns Gebrent ibber al hot men uns . . .

Similia similibus (tetraktos)
MATRONA
YHVH
AHVH (Love)

You will first find a cutlery.
Help yourself to the blade
most sinister.
Next, avoid the seething pot:
it is the smell of semen or of blood
shed in a murder.

These — a cenotaph
of spectacles, crockery shards,
rosewood phylacteries
are the tokens to guide your way
back across the trespass that is your
history. So
you must learn to read them
backward and even acrostic.

Electricity stutters in the bulb
and now a new dread rising,
older than the gods older than any
tribal medulla, whose emblems
are a headlouse
the spitted kid
a snakeskin nailed to the wall
will dog your last steps
to the door where —

a revolving head with
braziers for eyes, flame-crowned
in amethyst, teeth
of the sky's lapis lazuli
and I beat them as small
as the dust of the earth
I stamped them like the
mire of the street
doorpost-high and the dooryard
    behind
and holy smokes, what've I gotten
myself
into now?

With good bronze in the right hand let each of you slaughter sheep forever.
Homeric Hymn to Apollo,
l. 535

Whosoever shall make like unto that, to smell thereof, he shall be cut off from his people.   *Exodus 30:38*

When you come to the place of the pure marlbe stones do not say "Water, water."
Hekhalot Rabbati

Between the yea and the nay the heads are lopped off and the spirit takes flight.
Ibn 'Arabi

They will offer water from the river, do not take the water of death. They will give you grain from the fields of the dead. Do not take the seed, only say to her, "Give us the corpse that hangs on the spike."
Nippur tablet

The thigh of heaving and the breast of waving shall they bring with the offerings of the fat made by fire, to wave it for a wave-offering before the LORD YHVH and it shall be thine . . .   *Leviticus 10:15*

And he said unto me: 'This is the place where the priests shall boil the guilt-offering and the sin-offering, where they shall bake the meal-offering . . .'
Ezekiel 46:20

You who revoke decrees, undo vows, remove wrath, soothe fury, recall love, re-

---

R. Huna said: The doughs of a heathen, a man may fill his stomach with them, providing that he eat as much as an olive of unleavened bread at the end. Only at the end, but not at the beginning. What is the reason? Because he had not afforded it any guarding. Then let him guard it from the baking and onwards? Hence this surely proves that we require guarding from the beginning. Yet whence? Perhaps it is different here, because when guarding became necessary he did not guard it. But where he did guard it when guarding became necessary, it may indeed be that the guarding of the kneading is considered guarding. Yet even so, Raba did not retract. For he said to those who handled sheaves: Handle them for the purpose of the precept. This proves that he holds we require guarding *ab initio*, From beginning to end. Mar the son of Rabina, his mother stored grain for him in a trough. . . .
Our Rabbis taught: One may not mash a dish on Passover, and he who wishes to mash, must put in the flour and then add the vinegar. But some say, He may even put in the vinegar and then add the flour.
Who is 'some say'? Said R. Hisda, It is R. Judah. For we learned: A stew pot or a boiling pot which he removed

---

And even the palace is an elaborate artifice, a many-storied sand mandala, the work of a novice demiurge : every colored grain itself englobing an iridian universe.

store friendship before the splendor of the glory of the Dread One.
Why is it that sometimes you take fright and at other times you are merry? Why is it that sometimes you exult

seething, he must not put spices therein, but he may put them in-to a dish or tureen. R. Judah said: He may put them into any-

Ten Sephirot Beli-Mah perceived as if lightning—their aim has no end. Its utterance in them as a going forth and a return. And when its word is like the tempest they descend before the throne and they regale.
Sepher Yetsira I, 6

God is the answer, I agree. The question is, what is the question?

METATRON
MATRONA
concentricities
on concentricities of power
that may take the form even of three
tailors, talking shop:
Senoy, Sansenoy and Semangelof,
sartorially speaking

Eli, Eli!
Angelos thanatou
mengele in the jungele.

Then for the door to open repeat the formula: *parhedros*
For that art thou.

From the very headwaters of time my soul was hidden in his storehouse brought forth from nothing *but at the end of time I shall be summoned back before the King.* My life flowed out of the depth of the spheres which gave me form and order. Divine forces shaped me *to be treasured in the chambers of the King.*

ADDEXTRA
PATRIS:CHE
RUBINSTAT
CVNCTIPO
TENTIS

A tangled skein unperplexed by my monodies.

RaMBaM walks with RaBaD in the shade. RaMBaN confers with Moses de Leon.

Entrance of the Myrrhophores, Bearers of Myrrh. Queer to depict of all things a dance on a frieze. A frozen. Queerer to portray an aroma in relief: on the walls and queerer yet, prefigured as it were on the very ivory box of Myrrh they bore, whose entrance at this juncture of the Mysteries was preceded by the wafting incense: and so in a sense bore themselves in consequence before the Queen, twofold goddess Demeter-Persephone, mother and daughter born unto herself, whose significance the initiates could barely bear, in the context, that is, at this juncture of the Mysteries, Eleusinian, hallucinogenic, but that to us outside the context seems, well, merely queer.
twenty-two *autiot*, all told. . . . *nativus Nativot*
the inborn way

Quickly
confound him then
from your subtle store
of alphabetic secrets,
the seventy-two
hidden names
adding up to
METATRON
producing at last from your sack
the last petrifying glyph
to supplant him there
beneath the lintel.

Beyond are the tended olives
insects lacing the vines
the kitchen midden the shambles
the cluttered rooftiles
basking in all that sky.
Hens are scratching
their secret gematria
in the dust. Rabbis
garbed in the sanbenito
                stack
        loud argument
        for kindling: with
the wiry bean
and the fluted palm
soon their lamentation too
will ascend in slow spirals . . .
Meanwhile

the day's peristalsis
has loomed the serpent
a new garment, dazzling
against white stucco.
He instructs you
in soft sephardic fricatives —
Gaze out.

and at other times you are terrified? They said: 'When the face of the Divine Majesty grows dark, we stand in great terror. But when the sparks of the Shekhinah radiate, we are full of mirth!' from the *Greater Hekhalot*

4 palatial palatals
4 gutterals of the gutter
5 dentals sharpened to a point

The center is the threshold.
Jabès, *Return to the Book*, 194

Three Mothers: Aleph, Mem, Shin.
    Based on (a way, a foundation)
    hollow of the hand empty hollow
    of the hand full and what lies
    between: the tongue kneeling.
Sepher Yetsira III, 1

[H]e shall not return by way of the gate whereby he came in.
Ezekiel 46:9

He made his light to shine to bring her forth: to the right and to the left, each side hidden well-springs lay. He made her to descend the steps leading down from *the Pool of Shela to the garden of the King.* Strengthen the feeble one, let her stand firm. And when all things return to their primal state make her pure as she rejoins the royal pavilion in the *orchard of the King.*

Nachmanides, 'Mustaja on the Fate of the Over-Soul'

Alte clamat Epicurus: 'venter deus meus erit, talem deum gula querit, cuius templum est coquina, in qua redolent divina, in qua redolent divina.' *Carmina Burana*, 211

PossidETIN
dESACRAM:
SERAFIN
SINISTRAM

ET:CLA
MANT

S̄S   Vide Taautos [Thoth-Hermes]
S̄S   (in Philo of Byblos fr. 4)

S̄

It is a well-known fact that the Master of the *Sefer Yetsira* described the right-hand side, Our Lady of Mercy

thing but vinegar or brine! Yet let us establish it as R. Jose, for it was taught, R. Jose said: He can soak them in vinegar, and the vinegar binds them? We know R. Jose [to rule thus] only when it is by itself, but not when it is in a mixture. 'Ulla said: Both the one and the other are forbidden, because, 'Go, go, thou Nazarite,' say we, 'take the most devious route, but approach not the vineyard.' R. Papa permitted the stewards of the house of the *Resh Galutha* [the Babylonian Exilarch] to mash a dish with parched grains. Said Raba: Is there anyone who permits such a thing in a place where slaves are found? Others say, Raba himself mashed a dish with parched grains.
Tractate Pesahim Ch.II (40a,b)

If one strains to seek perfection in a moment he has marred it.
Instruction of Amenope, 18

For our part, we use not words, but sounds full of energy. . .
[Asclepius] *Corpus Hermeticum, XVI*

I have accomplished the descent of these fifteen steps of darkness and the ascent of the steps of light, and he who sacrifices is himself the sacrificial victim. . . .
Zosimus of Panopolis *Fragmenta Graeca*, 107-13

and Compassion, as water, since everything needs water. And as the Master of the *Sefer Yetsira* described the right-hand side as water, so he described the left-hand side as fire.
Moses of Burgos, *Book of the Left Pillar*

Be thou as the obedient god Iconoclastes who carefully polishes form until he can see his own graven reflection and then demolishes it.

The mystery does not get clearer by repeating the question, nor is it bought with going to amazing places. Until you've kept your eyes and your waiting still for fifty years, you don't begin to cross over from confusion.

Rumi, *Killiyat-e Shams*, 1088

The aspirant will then have been made their initiate.

Where you stand, there stand all the worlds. Moses Cordovero

Four rabbis entered PARDES: Rabbi Akiba, Ben Zoma, Ben Azzai and Aher. One saw and died, the second saw and lost his reason, the third laid waste the young plants. Only Rabbi Akiba entered in peace and came out in peace.

Hagigah 14b

The honey dance in the electric hive, Love's larder.

In those days, at that time, I'd see you slink by, last of your tribe — loose bracelets, a figure like the aleph, you didn't make a sound.

To the dancer belongs the universe.

Wisdom [Hokhmah] makes its abode, just as the silkworm encloses itself, as it were, in a palace of its own production, an abode which is both useful and beautiful . . . an inhabited abode named Elohim [palatium regis.]

Zohar I. 15a-b

When the most Mysterious wished to reveal himself, He first produced a single point which was transmuted into a thought, and in this he executed innumerable designs and engraved innumerable engravings. He further engraved within the sacred and Mystic lamp a mystic and most holy design, which was a wondrous edifice issuing from the midst of thought. This is called *MI* [who], and was the beginning of the edifice, existent and non-existent, deep-buried, unknown by name. Zohar Ib

It is MALCHUT, the kingdom, the foundation here below of what is above.

Respondemos: Aneynu: Answer us,
God of Abraham— The one who answers us in the hour of grace. Answer us. Answer us, Fright of Isaac—The one who answers in the hour of anguish. Answer us, strong One of Jacob—Answer us, God of the Merkabah.
Petition from the *Selichot* liturgy

O Wondrous
blue
enamel, the
cultivation
of mind's
witness.
At frames edge —
always at
just the edge —
a girl will dance for you
the Sighted Termite
and the joyous Uncoiling Incense.
Her nostrils are springing
violets, grain
sprouting at her instep.
So it has come to this . . .

Later, when night's paralysis
sloughs all learning from you
she will come to you
in her saffron dress.
She will replace your tongue
with a bitter root,
she will close a sparrow
in your chest. Her touch
is both grief's own and
anaesthetic.

Corridors, alcoves, antechambers . . .

Where was it I was trying to get to?
Nevermind.
Blue labials are glued tight
to your eyelids.
The numberless unkempt stars
cluster around your ears.
(A song of ascents)

The trickery goes further. The voice of the fire tells the *truth*, saying, *I am not fire. I am fountainhead. Come into me and don't mind the sparks.* Rumi, *Mathnawi V.*

The sanctuary at Pyla has two rooms, and over it reigns a two-headed Apollo. The first head is called *Lakeutes*; he presides over the fiery feast of sizzling meat and flaming flesh: a sonorous Apollo, whose music is the hissing of flames . . . the second epithet, *Mageiros* designates the god of butchers and cooks. Marcel Detienne

From Jericho did they smell the scent of the compounding of the incense. Said Eliezer b. Diglai, "My Father's house and goats were on the mountain of Mikhwar. And they sneezed from the smell of the compounding of the incense."

Tractate Tamid 3:8

'To the universe belongs the dancer….'
'Amen.'

Acts of John

The vessel I see now is much stronger than the one I saw earlier, and it will never fall or break.

Hildegard to Manegold, letter 122

. . . The desire arose from thought to extend itself, and it extended itself from the place where thought is concealed, which is unknowable until it spread and settled in the throat, the place that gushes continuously through the mystery that is the breath of life, and then once this thought had extended itself and settled in this place, thought was called "Living God". . .

Zohar I. 74a.

*Isis lactans : Salis sancti
Veni sponsa de Libano*

O glittering starlight, O most splendid and special form of regal marriage, O shining gem: you are adorned like a noble lady who has no blemish. And you are a companion of angels and a citizen among the saints. Flee, O flee the cave of the old betrayer and come, O come into the King's palace.

Hildegard of Bingen,
Symphoniae harmoniae celestium revelationum

What mean the words, 'after the manner of daughters'? It is a secret held solely in the trust of the wise! A palace which is known as the Palace of Love sits amidst a vast rock, a most secret firmament. Here in this place the treasures of the king are kept, and all his kisses of love.

Zohar

Again the halls, monasteries, palaces and pavilions are spontaneous apparitions all adorned with the seven jewels and hung with curtains of various other jewels, such as pearls and moonbright mani-gems.

The Larger Pure Land Sutra, 16.

Oh, give me the kisses of your mouth, for your love is more delightful than wine. Your ointments yield a sweet fragrance, your name is like fine oil — therefore do maidens love you. Draw me after you, let us run! The king has brought me to his chambers. Let us delight and rejoice in your love. Savoring it more than wine — like new wine they love you!

Song of Songs

The Absinthe Drinker

Los extremos se tocan, outside
at a bar in Barcelona
the sort of place where one can
ruin oneself
go mad
commit a crime — you know the sort —
and in fact about two purse-snatchings
per hour, approximately,
across the colonnaded courtyard,
roughly a seven second sprint.

And with each second some six-hundred million tons of hydrogen
are transmuted to helium in the sun
with the simultaneous conversion of four million
tons of matter into — energy? beverage? I forget what.

Put it down to absinthe-mindedness.

Dear Theo,
Thought I'd say more about this libation, dear to Artemis,
and illegal in every civilized corner of the world:

"They that regard lying vanities forsake their own mercy."
Allow me a nautical analogy:
Imagine one day finding quite by chance
that the mind is a "submersible."
At first you dabble with the odd plunge
into *errantry* and *melancholia,* losing yourself
in the shape-lit forests of kelp. But after a while
it's the bathos of bathysphere, and you're getting
spooked a bit by the noctiluca, lantern fish,
phantasms of the subconscious floating up.
And the grandiose of the ocean floor
littered with skeletal triremes and amphorae
and limpet-encrusted torsos of bronze.
Soon claustrophobia accommodates a solipsism:
you've been down for weeks now in the *Nautilus,*
somebody's misplaced the charts, and that constant

intercom in your head is none other than Captain Nemo, and he's
on a bender, recounting all his misadventures . . . So it was
with me, till out of the belly of megalomania I cried.
And my solipsism grew sick of itself and vomited me out
on the dry land.

What does this have to do with anything?
I'm getting to that. But first, excuse me, I have to
see a man about a dog.

The mothball. The latrine-lozenge.
The marble impediment.
Well-echoed wall tile
and obstinate elocution —
The reign insane
falls mainly on the pain.

I'm back.

Now first it's the look of it that gets you.
Not the green of renewal,
the sapling of verdure. No, not that at all.
Rather the malevolent, entirely
the green of a human venom.

But after the water — ah,
it's the eastern horizon just after
the sun drops in the west.
The antique celadon of the absolute.

Barcelona's a diurnal rotisserie.
Under the indefatigable, the high the annealing noon, when
all things hold their shadows in
like a breath held
the way you might to see somebody
jump from a burning absolute.
Slowly then they let 'em out.

'We should not drink this *veneno de serpiente,*'
says my aged drinking buddy.
'Better some wine. A good Penedès.
Reddens the ears, not the eyes,'
as from under his projecting beret
he lets out a long solicitous belch,
then ponders in silent eructomancy.

'Very Erasmical of you. Erasmical? Erasmusical?'

'Erasmian, Desiderius Erasmus, née Geert Geerts.'

I'm usually impressed by just what this old radical knows
and let him know it but just now
my tongue has grown numb
and peninsular. All else in a velvet halcyon of sorts, becalmed
in a wide sargasso of the mind. And suddenly—
post-impressionist.

'Things are really starting to progress.
From Degas to Cézanne, just like in the art history
books.'

'Ah, Cézanne. The almost, howdoyousay, *tactile* science
of his *passage.'*

'Palette tectonics.' Puns don't translate I find.
Now we're the only ones, except for the mad dogs
and Englishmen. And their wives and their beckoning purses.
Another round, the warm taste of reactor run-off.
With a twist of Good 'n Plenty.
It's a serenade for minds.
It's a moonlight lemonade.
Once the prostitute's swain of rich chrysolite.
At the state dinner it held sway
over the heads of distant potentates.

Now things have really gone,
from early Cubism to high Polyhedralism.
An image impinging:
flexible jumping beans
subtend the Angel of Incidence.
Very post-neo-cortical.

'Ramón, I think I'm seeing orgone maybe.
Or maybe it's electrons whizzing in their orbits.'

'No pasarán.' Off in his own world now, getting animated.
'No pasarán!' and raises the fist of solidarity.
'I was with Durruti. I was with the best!'

Elsewhere sunflowers will be hanging their heads
beneath an unenigmatic and Andalucian sky,
the mortar where daily choicest emeralds
are ground for pigment. I'm suddenly
understanding Catalan.

Tell me, pale Ramón,
Does the ice floe know
        it is by its own element ferried
            towards a more temperate meridian?
And does the drinker of wormwood?

The Analects of Lady Mondegreen (3)

Cement will dry if you let it
Beware of the wooly stink
There are more than two facts
Mince pie is a dish served to children

Beware of the wooly stink
The pastrami also gives shame
Mince pie is a dish served to children
They get their kicks from buckets of swill

The pastrami also gives shame
The wall phone rang wild and possum
They get their kicks from buckets of swill
Smile when you say *nasty*

The wall phone rang wild and possum
A wax floor makes for a smooth balance
Smile when you say *nasty*
Flax makes a fine brand of paper

A wax floor makes for a smooth balance
Light evil makes for a small room
Flax makes a fine brand of paper
She blushed when he gave her a light-orchid

Light evil makes for a small room
The girl at the booth sold fifty bombs
She blushed when he gave her a light-orchid
The last switch cannot be turned off!

The girl at the booth sold fifty bombs
The Peace League met to discuss their plans
The last switch cannot be turned off!
Her purse was filled with useless trash

The Peace League met to discuss their plans
The carnie girl took off her hat
Her purse was filled with useless trash
Note closely the size of the gas tank

The carnie girl took off her hat
The junkyard had a funky smell
Note closely the size of the gas tank
The cable room stank before meals

The junkyard had a funky smell
His strong arm shall shield your honor
The cable room stank before meals
He sliced the shellfish sideways

His strong arm shall shield your honor
The muff is stylish once more
He sliced the shellfish sideways
He asks a new person to vouch for him

The muff is stylish once more
Mate for life with more than one
He asks a new person to vouch for him
After the dance the restraining order

Mate for life with more than one
The place seems dull and vegetable
After the dance the restraining order
We need an end to all such matters

The place seems dull and vegetable
There are more than two facts
We need an end to all such matters
Cement will dry if you let it

Fit the Second

How Small Brides Survive in Extreme Cold

Complainte:

Night in the rain.
A vertical loom.
A ten-thousand-stringed instrument.
Eighty-four thousand frets. Moreover
and more to the point I
can't help noticing
the singular touch of the demiurge
about it, that sonic
          maundering
the virtual verisimilitude
of random licks
          and those signature
wing-tipped sferics of his —
gatling-stratocaster-canticles-
cum-cumulo-static-antiphon
          the very likes of which . . .
Scaling the extremities of invention.

(Over my shoulder the Muse clears her
throat.) What — have I
committed an anthropomorphism?
Consider then some typical
prodigies and freaks of physics
drawn from the cabinet of curiosities
as yet inexplicable,
pyrotechnics like
"jets" and "sprites"—
red jellyfish of plasma
spouting thirty miles above
the cloud line, dangling
eerie green
tentacles of ion.
Consider sympathetic discharge
across isolated storm systems
some two hundred miles apart.
To the awed cosmonaut taking it all in from Mir

it appears, how do you say, choreographed after a fashion,
like telluric bolshoi, like orgone luminating —
and somehow eerily familiar,
a childhood glimpse
of intricate firefly synchrony,
vouchsafed and forgotten.
Or like fresh pang of *nostalghia,*
the neurons of remote cortices
calling to one another
across the corpus callosum . . .

Unnerved, he averts his gaze,
scrutinizes instead for some
human artifact, a scarcely
visible scar on the face of Asia.

So, on the one hand, anthropomorphism,
the human drama projected on a storm.
Then on the other — anthropocentrism,
the reflex, the baby-grip that
clings to consciousness as a birthright,
our own and ours only. From arrogance, I guess,
but moreso, fear. Terror of the kinship
terror in a lab rat's eye, half his brain
exposed and wired, terror of our own exposure
to the demon-haunted verge,
beset on all sides and nothing but
our ideologies to avert it — don't get me started —
the way for example our empiricism
walls up an empire within the humanly visible —
though we know full well it's but the
merest impress, just a notch really
scored across an astronomical spectrum . . .

And so tonight perhaps
at long last, the millennial din
of that last ptolemaic
crumbling in on itself
in decaying orbits. (What was it Hegel said
about the Owl of Minerva?)
All the while I'm going on like this

raptored gusts lash the panes
as a monodical and distinctly phrygian
wailing takes up with the fretful gnashing of sash
and starts to modulate
intoned as it were,
as though a frayed angel
were on the ledge
keening.
(Surely it is Uriel,
one of Those Who Watch,
he it is who is over clamor
and terror)
and it won't let me get an edge in wordwise.
Demiurges, angelologies —
this is what you get for reading
the *Book of Enoch* at four in the A.M.

At just this point of the vigil,
the ninth in as many nights,
a something
a small noumenon
summoned up by my obstreperous
right temporal lobe maybe,
approaching
stealthily and from behind —
my every numbered hair on end —
      crept up
      repent
      on all fears
      my spine
and swivelling 'round found myself
face to face
with none other than, *mirabile dictu:*
      the In-its-elf.
(You know, I always felt a twin —
I don't know how to say this . . .
the number eleven — it has
such an "elven" sound, and when
she left I felt
pth . . . phth . . . a twine-thin
wand

stranded on my tongue.)

Time now whence to take it all down
before I succumb once more to the Quartan Quotidian,
that ague of acquaintance I've grown to know
as the Grip, a.k.a. Dr. Lockjaw,

the duct that leach the dolce
from out the far niente . . .

(Don't dramatize these anxieties.
Geometrize 'em:
difficulties squared by despair,
the potent of exponent, or rounded,
like the Cape of Good Hope.)

Well, more phantasms and mythologems
still: the deafening clangor you hear
percolating up from the basement —
that would be the shade
of Ludwig van again
going at it on the heating pipes —
who else could summon such tympany
from aught but madness
and a monkey wrench? Moreover
and more to the plaint, the gripe
and distress of this "radiator," like the
bunged intestine of Industry.
Eloi, Eloi, Spasmodic Moloch!
Syncopate me Nobodaddy! With a
chorus as old as homo habilis, a
relentless mental flint-knapping,

till you swear you can feel the planet's velocity
feather-weight on the scalp
grosse fuge in your gut.

Any wonder that
when it lets up
I get the hell out?

A sord of mallards.
A murmuration of starlings.
A prating of goldfinches
darting one by one away
from where the shadbush blooms
in time for the yearly run
its namesake makes
up the obstacle course of the Connecticut,
and in the distance a whine of semis
hydroplaning the interstate, sounding
exactly like an angry hive.

Anyway, this is where
I'd intended to end it,
the poem I mean or rant or whatever it is
(my minimum poetics — can't be both)
and so spare you the reader and these the trees
(working title: 'Notes From the Underground:
Beethoven and the Metro Gnome')
but no soap — now I feel a leavening
of the theme coming on: a book of hours
of sorts, the seasons and their attendant
occupations, ostensible bucolics —
I once knew a shepherdess
named Scarlet Amaryllis. From Amarillo,
Texas no less.
Semi-classical
salon nude
composition. Preoccupied I
step into these
the woods, and into deepest folkloric
odors, residues fungal and coniferous,
the nearly visible effluvium of thaw.
It appears that I vanish
into the trees, but really
it's the other way around.

Our Lady of Solitude,
numerously titled
Mother and Muse,
You of Solace and Asperity,

Compassioness and sternest Archon,
Creatrix, Meretrix, Matrix,
Queen Nepenthes,
if ever I have merited your favor,
if I have put myself in harm's broad way
ever and over again by way of service
to your parlous rule, disdain not then
my presumptuousness here
and withhold not I pray your
charmèd vocables, to whatever
tokening they may lead.
Just then it dawns on me.

1

On Paradise Pond
two drops
spell the widening vowels of sorrow.
Twenty more or so strung on a web,
another clinging to a pendent bud
of saxifrage
in which a world swims.

It is April and still leafless,
morning and still forbidding,
and all along this stretch of the Mill
reflected oaks maple sycamore
are pulsating
            intricately, I
can't help but notice, like ganglia
lost in thought.

An aging army cargo plane
drags its sorry mass
and its sack of rumble after
halfway 'cross the infinite.

Eight somethings, ducks I think
by the whistling of their wings,
fly over, reconfigure
(four and four then five and three).

As above so below —

a descending cessna
drone in a gyre
and its circling virtual
grip all the isomorphic pieces of the scene
in a sort of upward fall —
and me between,
suspended in the inverted vertigo
it engenders, struggling
to take it all down
particular by particular,

as if it mattered somehow,
as if somehow the ineffable
had finally been effed —
though on further reflection
every choice every word of course
occludes another, in other words,
feckless maundering
no matter what angle you work it.
Speaking for myself, the jargon's
too flimsy, my architectonic
too coarsely woven for the task,
as when the mesh is more capacious
than the fish. This place is
fairly rife with awareness,
but my own, up all night, keeps vacillating,
past and future
the obvious and the oblivious
and the scarcely registered —
this stippling of light
so, I don't know, cantabile
from node to node
a music which won't get put to words.
And the lambent of it an amber net
cast on the bottom silt.

Tergiversate or not tergiversate
that is the question
          punctuated by fiddleheads

unfurling underfoot, iterant
in that trimming banner of geese
quodlibet overhead and the
pockets of tepid air contending with the cold.

It is April in the marches of Massachusetts,
the very cusp of spring.
Between the brief parentheses
of a lunation.
If one proposition is affirmed
all others will follow suit.

It can go either way, I figure.
No words not even paradox
can fix as equivocal a presence as this.

2

Every word occludes another, just as
every perspective cuts across
some larger circuitry — logjams
of purposiveness, the whole farrago
of incidence, everything a something
taken out of context, the stunned minnow
in the heron's crop
mouthing the vowels of *horror,* or the way
you wake up sometimes with a
loded word on the tongue
the odd fragment
of dream cipher (today no
kidding it was *tatterdemalion*).

But of the mechanism, spring-
wound, that drives these recirculating
waters, disgorged on the hill towns in
last night's storm or unlocked
from the rockface its last
blue icicle integument, trundling
past stubborn milltowns and
former milltowns, their trestles
cantilevers and

crumbling abutments,
their sullen smokestacks,
rosettes of identical split-
level around the cul-de-sac,

sluiced through the archaic reactor
whose lab-coated acolytes
scrutinize the apparatus, tending
the device
its dread core their queen
hived and bloated with light,

turning bend after bend
of perturbation to get here
where the currents slow to spread their snares
and drop their sediment —
we are all of us oblivious,
taken in entirely by the parade
of forms, the events and detritus
that drift across the meniscus of consciousness.
Only the sandpiper it seems
sees past its own reflection —
and the kingfisher, who lunges now
through the shattered pane
to that low strange corridor
its glimpse of minnow where
last year's leaves in a
spectral cortege, lit
with the amber half-light
of the after-life
leach their tannins or settle
little by little a skeletal tracery
into the bottom silt,
thick as the dust of an undisturbed
necropolis.

While above an unseen hand works feverishly
to smooth the sheet of other-being
over the ever-unmade bed of the river.

And while I'm going on like this
a something noses closer through the shallows,
something I didn't notice, nor
he me til
thwack
and recoil
the beaver startled startles back
his blackjack tail on the water's pate
then
thwack again
          KERTHUNK
in spreading rose-windows
of concussion. The Willow-Manitou
looks on and marvels.
An after-sprite of droplets shivers down.

Several weeks now he's been at it
this waterlogged carpetbagger
interloping both the banks up and down.
Daylong the air endures the rasp
and crepitation of his handiwork, a
jigsaw of precision, each chiselled branch
a deftly-placed sprag in the works.

For these two are pitted
here and everywhere
one against the other:
the curving intelligence of river,
the Cartesian architectonic
of the beaver, part iconoclast
breaking the symmetries,
troubling the face of the waters, part
masonic artificer, geometrician,
master anaesthetician, plotting and fretting
to put the river under and
three or four in confederacy
equal to an entire
army corps of engineers.

But for now the river doesn't give a damn.
Rather it is the dam that gives.

And so on and so forth through the spate of May . . .

Days wax expansiver.
Time slides by.
Mid-month,
middle of the way.
I'm making for the cowfield,
the hill and its stump,
navel of Northampton.
Already the scene is swamped
in the competing ranks of
sumac, mullein and burdock.
A grain silo
a couple of antique smokestacks
a white steeple
needling the absolute —
these and the rooftops of the
abandoned mental hospital
being the last vestiges of human artifact
to rise above it.

Distance spreads itself
across the scrim of all things,
sets the stage on which
giddiness
          lifts the bridal veil
laying bare what is called
delectatio summi, the delight of height,
which is a state of mind.
Bodies just do what bodies
do best — they fall.
This is called "the melancholy of anatomy."
(As if in disproof of the principle
countless swallows ply the sky
harrowing heaven with the descant of their ascent.
While a few, flying too close to the wings
are snatched from the scenery by an
unseen hand.)

Why then skip ye hills like lambs,
ye coverts like the ramping goats?

Because of what Democritus calls
clinamen: the atomic swerve,
that node of sudden impetus and spontaneity.
The weft of what is otherwise warp.
Otherwise everything rushing
every which way
away from everything else —
this is called the universe.
Everywhere is center with every redshifting else
fleeing it as fast as it
possibly can,

compounding its centrality with distance
in coarse simulacrum of the infinite.

Westron wind. Anon. in love.
Locust-scented petalfall.
Soon it's coming down like there's
no tomorrow — mutatis mutandis
whirled without end, everywhere
raining catalpas and dogwoods!

3
In the perennial garden all riot
is to its proper bed assigned and properly
labeled, as it was in the beginning
in our first garden, when God
took Adam by the hand
and was instructed in the names.
Obliquely we walk in the cool of the day
striving to recover them.

Heartsease, *Viola tricolor*
a wild pansy also known as
Johnny-jump-up, and Love-in-idleness.

Trillium grandiflorum, the Wake-Robin
of E. North America, a "distinctive whorl
of three leaves, with a solitary white
or red flower."

Arisaema dracontum, Green Dragon,
"Characteristic of the arum family,
the green spadix protrudes from a hooded spathe."

Lapsana communis, Nipplewort,
Adlumia fungosa, Climbing Fumatory,
Penstemon hirsutus, Hairy Beard-tongue.
Green Turban
Marlinspike
Episcopal Miter

And here, Golden Marguerite.
My botanical guidebook glosses it thus:

"It would have taken a Bach to compose this species . . .
Notice the way the sepals provide 'quasi-continuo'
accompaniment to the corolla's demisemiquaver
figuration. It is said the formal panoply of the universe
may be discriminated in its latticed flowerhead . . . . an induced
sostenuto, by the which place rhymes with time:
a sestina divided by a villanelle."

(Meantime,
between the brief parentheses
of a lunation, how the river rises and falls,
like a fever chart.
Drowsy thrush music.
Berries grow dropsical
in the rank haze of generation and corruption.
A strangulation of honeysuckle,
a quandary of humans huffing and jogging by,
a jewelled dragonfly, *Anax junius,*
Lord and Master of June —
a.k.a. the Darning needle, Snake Doctor —
hawking from stalk to stalk, sunlight
beading through the tracery of nervure
along its wings, and my own
fever swollen, watching me from a distance
knee-deep amid the bracken.)

Over here another favorite,
Papaver somniferum:

"On slenderest stalk
the poppy, rose's antidote,
poses its singular paradox:
to be the velvet-appointed catafalque
of uneasy dreams
draped in the crêpe of awakening."

       4

Praise the mantled dignity of roots,
those humble nodes, Hermetic caches
symbolic of thrift and hidden store,
repository of heavy elements and other dross
looted from a star's demise:
      fatted yams
      mandrake autochthons
      tuber dirigibles
      drifting through the dark of loam,

      the grub-colored
      parsnip I wit-
      nessed, more
      stubborn and
      longer by a
      head than
      the yankee
      gardener
      who labor-
      ed three
      whole days
      to prise
      its ta-
      pering
      grip —

      and don't forget the
      mangel-wurzel,
      its moral ambiguity
      and Freudian undertones.

Praise the strive and grapple of roots,
those buried muscles of thrive and gathering dominion.
The elm with one sure tendon
cracks a sidewalk eighteen feet away,
by inches hurls the pavement
as it would surely heave
the goddamn continental plates
given time and tenure.

And not just roots, by Hades, but praise
all creatures of the underworld.
Though our typic abode of the dead,
it is in fact now known that pound for pound
more organisms live below the ground than on
or above it. Still others are inhumed to be reborn.

Behold the burrowing hornworm
down in the bone midden among
bottleglass, mouse tibiae,
crockery and arrowheads, putting by
his last good suit, his single thorn
for this sarcophagus of basalt, bossed
with the effigy not of what he was
but of what he is molding into, the
sphinx moth imago emergent.

                 5
Now I the shrill-voiced cicada sing!
who lives one frantic summer's fortnight
in the air — and that after
thirteen or seventeen occulted years
in servitude to Persephone,
blindly plumping at the root,
a white kernel that is sweetening —
treat for a mole!

This is the goal of all living:
to be the thing that splits its shell
to become the beguiling bull-roarer
of the child Dionysos,

to hollow out an hour with incessancy
and punctuate a calendar
with dithyramb.
To be the wound coil
and summa of a season.

6

It is a huge hybrid something-or-other
half orchid half pudendum from
Hell's own hothouse and reeking
of the most sexual Latin, the eloquent
vulgate you find yourself speaking
sometimes in dreams. Antediluvian
madder lake more or less
on a ground of alabastrine.
Undulating sepals and a labellum
that beetles o'er its base.
Something's not kosher in Elsinore.
On closer inspection I notice
this minute homunculus of a botanist
straddling a stamen and peering back
at me. (Such infestations
are not unheard of, most notably
in the cultivated specimens. Though
without visible means of sustenance,
this botanist would have survived like
others of its kind, sucking facts from the
host plant, much of which it regurgitates
back to its young.) His voice is so small:
I think he said 'Artaud',
though when I ask again it sounds
more like 'Ars artem falleret',
or perhaps 'Theophrastus Bombastus me fecit,'
I assume a sobriquet. Wait — I'd
almost forgotten — rummaging through I
manage to produce a
magifying glass from my burglar's kit.
His eyes are sad and of a mansuetude,
his antics, well, unwonted.
On closer scrutiny I notice

the antebellum vade mecum that lies
open on his lap.
Its title:
"How Small Brides Survive in Extreme Cold."
And there I read
(moonscape within a moonscape)
the ruined portico and the rain,
the catbird
        its variations on no theme,
the wandering fountain
        trailing its vines and jasmines,
and you, gracing a window:
        surd of a magnitude,
        my marble alibi,
        Eidolon, Eidolon . . .
Caryatid of my dream temple.

Yes, I know I'm desperate.
And yes, I musta got some kinda cojones
breaking into the greenhouse and all.
But tell the truth, I'd sooner bring you
a cabbage for corsage, than snip a blossom
of *Cattleya Catullus.*

7

What gramarye is this
what nimble prestidigitation
that the least part should conjure up
the whole witching season?

One red stem of a yellow leaf seen
through the warped pane of a grid that is
grease-smoked on the inside, the outside
streaked with light,

the one red stem so slight
one wonders how it could be
so blatantly looming — the blunt
insistence of the fuse

in the very instant
of using itself up, of losing
itself to the impending
pandemonium —

and how could it be
so damn articulate
to pick it from the ruck
in the middle of all that maple-

self-despoiling, propping
a sallow fond farewell —
salutation following on salutation —
and decipher its reiterate semaphore,

to wit: *wand love* —
writ in the elemental morphemes
of mentalese — summoning
in its disappearing act

the implicate weft
the reticulate nervure
of beings
of what is bound up in intricacy

particular by particular —
shuttling back and forth,
woof of the larger loom it implicates
by way of sympathetic magic,

by way of offering itself up, self-
condemned, an auto-auto-da-fé
fanning its own flame
to wave it for a wave-offering

before succumbing to the general hecatomb
and tumult, and somersaulting away
in the wavering so-long
of the after-blue.

8

A sand shovel is waving in cloudless space,
a ship is sailing absently by,
sand drifting in runnels of itself
or spilling absently from a pail.
Sound of breakers stumbling,
salutation following on salutation.

It is now we learn to decipher them
or never,
the worn reliefs on
memory's alabaster,
a clouding lucency.
In November, when Remember and her brood
come home to roost
in a cleft
in your conscience, o my reverie.

9

Two wheels ordain our days,
between these two our separate ways.
One winches on the rack of time —
Kalachakra in the Sanskrit —
every breath another ratchet.
So finely is its calibrating
you hardly feel the fibers rending.

The other eddies retrograde
and to the dulling of the blade.
Rimless, naveless and unspoken,
mentioned only as "Akin"
and only once in all the fragments.
By *attention* it is turned,
as every breath more hurdy-gurdy

draws all things in its convolving
hastening the ricercar

till aether turns to flint
and busted planets trace

their course to fire . . .
Aldebaran shrinks back, the Pleiades
and the Beehive Cluster.

To the timbrels of faintest crickets
the tremble and groan of axle
a terrible engine approaches,
Torquemada device,
as molecule by inexorable molecule
Paradise Pond submits
to the mechanism of ice.
Somewhere across the water
I can hear the beaver still
gnawing away at the dark.
I picture him there
a demiurge a tatterdemalion —
with fur slicked back to points
the darkness oozing out of,

teeth
        honed and yellowed
as the moon's
        own incisor —
gnawing to carve
intricate headpost
for the riverbed.

10

In winter it's the labels only that survive,
stalks of tin among the stubble
casting blue shadows on the snow
where creatures leave their signatures
and heave their blackness through the air.
The placards are embossed with appellations —
Latin binomial, then common or cognomen,
and region of origin if given —
and gone all traces of their bearers
buried in the drifts.

'Why look — a flower cemetery.'
'You'll notice,' I insinuate, 'how this scene
resembles the poem containing it, all poems,'
the alabaster vocables flaking off,
snaking away into breath-smoke.
'Hmm. Metaphor as metaphor.'
'Or metaphor *for* metaphor:
prajñaptimatra in *madhyamika*-speak,
all "things" existing as mere designations.'
'Well, metaphor for metaphor, how's about this:
poetry is a passing, lone, slightly discomfited
elephant, scratching its butt on an abandoned
termite mound. No one quite remembers when
civilization checked out — maybe the queen died,
or a badger sacked it — but the elephant
keeps this place in mind and comes by when he can,
just for the simple delectation of it. . .'
(Bill stoops to read a tag, while I chew a few more
of the Jimsonweed seeds we'd collected earlier
from the pods.)
'*Asclepias verticillata*, Linear-leaved milkweed —
hey, wait a minute! You know, I believe we've
stumbled onto — no shit — the lost Necropolis of the Archetypes.
Look here: *Pulmonaria*, "Mrs. Moon," Lungwort.
And here: *Endymion non-scriptus*, English Blue-bell.
Don't you get it? The tutelary forms and mythemes
of antiquity, long since sunk into inconsequence.'
'Reduced to inscription. *Asphodeline lutea*,
Asphodel, King's Spear. DIS MANIBUS.
I confess, though, I would have expected a
"sublimer" ethos, broad Alyscamps, elegiac statuary,
something more De Chirico or Père Lachaise.'
'Too obvious. Anyhow they're not really dead,
or even forgotten. It's just that the ur-myths are
portmanteaued into the urban myth. To find them
you only gotta pick up the Weekly World News.'
'You know, I feel the datura kicking in . . .
Forget the Weekly World News, I have
my own shocking prognostications: In this
the millenarian year of twenty-aught-naught
I foresee . . . certain celebrity unions on the rocks . . .

this book on the Index . . . finally, the truth
about Roswell . . . Armageddon won't bring about the end
of civilization as we know it — poetry will.
Vaunting the architecture state and status have
erected. Yet even now, rough pachydermal words
do smooth it back to dust.'
       'Back to mild protuberance of the Serengeti.'

Silently we trudge across the uncharted tundra
of the page, preoccupied — 'Hey, watch your step,'
(a still-steaming dog turd). Preoccupied
I stoop to a tag that catches my eye,
wipe away the obscuring rime,
deciphering,
        Omphalodes verna
           Creeping forget-me-not
   'It figures.'

11

A score of grackles on the wires
like the opening quarter notes of Magnificat.
Jeer of jay and the catbird's rigamarole.
It would take a Bach to compose this scene.

And so in bitterest February I proffer this:
snug in careful wording, skillfully wrought and beaten,
my opulent heart on silver salver, a valentine,
to be strung as a bauble, a trinket about your neck,
o my reverie,
Shekhina-Arethusa,
Our Lady of the Perpetual Leave-taking.

12

March. A long agonizing travail.
All night the crazed music coming down,
somebody, Elderhand of my own maybe,
thrumming the Storm Guitar.
Over by the fireplace, in place of a fire
a stone jar sits before the grate

with a mouth opening to a tangle of stalks
having just yesterday been brought in to be forced
and already burst into forsythia,
untimely and out of place.
At dawn it lets up and I get the hell out.

Fresh footprints the sleepwalker left
on the abandoned dooryard of Massachusetts.

My own places of trespass are these:
the derelict of a railroad bridge
(and the railroad ditch jammed with
early daffodil),
a stand of birch by the toolshed
where the old moon lodges
enmeshed in the interstices.
And lastly, that clearing
where the wheel ruts just end,
empoplared copse
sere and sedge
bordering the depopulated cosmopolis
of these pages (I can't help but
notice this glaring omission
of things human. So be it.)
Tilth and fallow, the earth by now
is fairly saturated with
promise,
hewn by thaw, riven by crocus,
and spiked with empurpled hyacinth.

Hysterico-tragical hyacinth —
Like an accident in the factory of wax pantaloons!

From back of the sun's front parlor
Seeps an odor of tapers in the moon's boudoir.

Trampled its philtres stain the snow,
Purest murex in the mountain pass:

The sight of it that Sappho likened
To a lost maidenhead.

Back at the cowfield, the stump omphalos.
A single bone, a femur,
Remains to mark the place
Where last year's fox carcass
Lay through all the stations of decay,
Better polished this morning
And more to the point
Than any Medici marble tomb
Or alabaster for that matter.

Epithalamium

Cherry Lane's what's known as the other woman.
Demimondaine thus, she resents her status:
and already psyched for the slots in Vegas,
lune-de-miel-wise.

His divorce comes through and she has to think fast.
First, a stratagem out of Lysistrata.
Then a false pretense, gets 'em both on TV,
airing his laundry:

that obsession with an equestrienne crop:
those unchaste requests for a kinky three-way;
can't yet get it up unless she performs first
(fancies a fan dance).

Once, a birthday gift dominatrix get-up.
Bernie now comes out and the tables are turned,
blabbing how they met and the sawbuck it cost.
(Over a lap dance.)

Music to the ears of the sponsors while the
censors are sweating his command of French which
thrills the audience, as it will the grandkids,
lip-reading "Chub-breath."

But the cards are stacked like a Vegas show girl.
Leastwise she had sense not to raise Viagra.
Springer's Final Thought, and her ultimatum,
sap his resistance.

Hurry, they'll hold the Liberace Chapel!
(Thus with vrai panache circumvents the pre-nup.)
Well defrocked or not, the guy's still a preacher.
Jesuit, hirsute.

He, a rented tux, with a cummerbund yet.
She, hubristic white, hudibrastic lipstick.
Slow and sodden steps between jaundiced bridesmaids.
Marmoset handshake.

Bubbly by the case, and a Sara Lee cake.
Nothin' is too good for his wife of twenty.
Then the bride stripped bare by her bachelors even,
tenders the fan dance.

Lines written upon encountering the ghost of Wittgenstein
on a precipice overlooking the symposium
honoring the centenary of his birth,
the night of the eclipse
Kirchberg am Wechsel, Nether Austria, August 1989

> *None may usurp this height, returned that shade,*
> *But those to whom the miseries of the world*
> *Are misery, and will not let them rest . . .*
> *Endymion*

Wolf clouds in sheep clothing
move in for the kill —

but the moon
  she eats cloud
    chomp
    chomp

deliriums dark and bodiless
wander the hills
while under the hills the philosophers
swarm and murmur

— "like the sound of an engine
 idling" — a visitant omygod
 beside me, lantern-
 faced, eye of a basilisk.

— Leapin' lizards! (I heard myself saying)
 Who, or what
 in Jove's name are you?

— I . . . I am the microcosm,
 (and it was then I knew)
 doomed for a certain term
 to wander the vast unheimlich of my thought.

— Well this is strange, to say the least,
I say as we begin to circumambulate
the dreadful summit and its church,
bearing, barely, the weight of its years,
a half millennium and then some,
its hide a pocked and luminous limestone,
its buttresses clutching the rock: a sphinx
on eighteen legs crouching —
that rounding a corner rears
a blank and questioning facade.

— "Of course it is strange,
     no longer to inhabit the earth,
     no longer to practice uses barely acquired,
     not to give meaning to roses
     and other typically promising things
     in terms of a human future.
     No longer to be the one that one was
     in endlessly anxious hands:
     to put aside even one's own name
     like a broken gamepiece . . ."
In truth, I miss damn little.
Schubert, yes —
the gothic rapacity of his
Death and the Maiden,
and the rest as well:
Meister Eckhart
in the guise of a balding bohemian.
Quite impossible to explain.

— Well perhaps then you can explain
     your thought and theory, which
     I have been butting my head up against
     these past nine years.

(The moon thinned to a wafer
as if for want of mass.
Exhalation
from the danker recesses
of the nave, where shadows crowd:
each shadow a niche withholding

each niche enfolding a saint
each saint hovering in a thought
each thought surrounded by a nimbus
blue and enigmatic.)

— I am not eager to rehearse these things.
   Hypothesi non fingo philosophorem,
   only points of view, of which
   these days I remember only two —
   the rest is just commentary,
   marginalia on marginalia.

— Namely?

— No, that's not quite it either.
   It's more of a way,
   leading to a point of view.

— So, "back to the rough ground," hmm?

— It is a way much like
   the one that brought you here —
   studded with shoulder blades
   of flint and the knuckles
   of oak roots
           crooked
   toward the underworld and meant
   to send you sprawling.

— It seems you've grown prolix with death.

— O.K. Firstly, a seeming conundrum:
   how and that we picture the world to ourselves
   shows how and that we cannot use language
   to get outside of itself. But the conundrum
   is just in the saying it.

— I can see how that remained
   a constant in your thinking,
   But language, it seems to me,
   is always getting outside of itself.

— Yes of course. But that *shows itself*.
   What shows itself cannot be said:
   I mean that careful holy thread
   between the twin beelzebubs
   mein und Meinen.

And here I guess we've gone
as far as we can go.
We attempt to chalk a boundary
around it, only to find
it has already and always
circumscribed us . . .

— And the second?

— is pretty much the same:
   "A philosopher stinks from the head down."

All around the trees
are twisted in grotesque
as if frozen in flight —
the devil's own topiary.
Suddenly the sphinx
lifts her facade
and speaks:

   You cannot name me
   without breaking me.

(Silence for a brief spell,
till he declaims,)

— The riddle does not exist!

A satyr canters across the path
crashes through the underbrush —
and the sphinx
before crumbling
back into church
casts aloft her handful of bats,
a gesture I take to mean

"many happy returns,"
but he retorts

— There will be no returns.

The moon above was in eclipse
and like unto a sack of blood
or a patch of dull lichen splayed
on the calcined headstone
of Necessity.

— I foresee a day
   and none too distant when
   propositions faltering
   are split down their Epimenides,
   all letters all but forgotten —
   but a final omega, emptied of content
   nailed like a hapless horseshoe
   to the butt-end of alphabet —
   and the whole of inarticulate creation ringing
   to a single benedictive
   "Yes." *Es müss sein.*

         A last bat in a slant
plies the sky
         quick
just clears the sextant of our thinking —

and he started like a scornful thing
upon an intolerable summons:
Magister Wittgenstein, agnostic gnostic,
apostate rabbi of the imponderable,

combining a talmudic subtlety of ken
with the fastidiousness of the priest
      who wipes and wipes
            every last atom of God
from out the holy calix —

Mañjusrï! brandishing
the flame-bound
          Occam's razor
to cleave the bonds of ego,
like a scalpel cutting its own edge.

A parting shout:
— Keep handy my *Tractatus*
    where I yet live on . . .
and he was gone.

The clouds thick, liturgical,
the moon a thurible swaying through.

Bats loop the loop
disappear
through the barred windows of church.

In Memory of Dr. Adolf Hübner

In the Golden Tea Hut of What

your absence sits beside me
just as you used to do.
A figment. An artefact.
A philosopher's prosthesis —
your absence is easy to conceive, mine
more difficult.

Acorns are knocking on the roof,
moonlight speculates across the floor,
while beneath the gilt, carpenter ants
tunnel their love.
We are each of us testing
as if by hypothesis
the Hutness of What.

You know how sometimes you can be oblivious
to something incessant until it lets up?
(The refrigerator's drone comes to mind,
the monotone of certain pains.)
These days the din of the late crickets
has been winding down
and often falters altogether —
after just about wearing my hearing away
awaiting word from you.
In their racket you can already detect
the thinning timbre of frost.

Here heaven and earth meet,
a lacquer lid snug on a lacquer box.
Beyond, valley folding into valley
folding into fog.
Slugs coupling, slimed leaves,
must of mast and what-have-you.
Ghost lights among the leafrot,
glowworms, foxfire and whatnot.
Killdeersong
to punctuate the heart.
A loss's only measure they say
is in the things that linger.

Here a pair of crook'd branches
to prop up the eaves, hardly
an inside from an out. And
between — a hushed attentiveness
ushers in to fill the gap,
just as you used to do.

Listen. You might nearly make out:
Poison-berries ripening on the Silence bush,
the far-off inaudible tom-toms
of the carpenter ants
(they are passing minutest palindromes
back and forth) — or subtler still,
the soft palaver of our sweet nothings.

'What have we here — split bamboo
whisk, rusting kettle, a sprig
of goldenrod — all the adornments of emptiness.
And this?'
      'Powdered hyson. Just the familiar
equipage, the same old same old.'
      'Indeed: two cups, even an ashtray.
It seems you've set a place here in my absence.'
      'Nothing is that doesn't seem, or so they say,
and cannot be but in its place.'
      'I beg to differ.'
      'Whad'ya mean?'
      'This absence business. It isn't a bit
a part of place. It is time and time again
what makes the difference that is itself.'
      'Leaving much
to be desired.'
      'Forced march, traipsing the legions of aeon . . .'
      'Well it takes two crows to make a murder.'
      'The more the harbinger, my dear.'
      'That hasn't prevented me from devising
an entire physics of absence. Check this out:
I call it a "desiderameter" — it's a sort
of sextant for gauging the compass of a longing.
I'm also re-calibrating it for use in Laconics.
That's the science of silences. But there it gets

a bit tricky — a simple pause, for example,
amplifies in breadth, depth, weight and volume
as it lengthens.'
    'I suspect because the longer it lasts
the more disquietingly it approximates the final pause,
that at the end of a life sentence.
Which reminds me — have you heard the one about
Plato's ark? One bird, one moon, and a single
chair to sit on.'
    'Which reminds *me* — how
the swallows all course in pairs
that vault of sky between the Palatine and
Capitoline hills — remember?'
    'Of course. And across the forum,
under the Domus Aurea,
Nero angles in the cloaca of darkness.
Are you getting this down? 'Cause
if it's tropes you want, well it's tropes I got,
aplenty. What else is a voice in your head good for?'
    'I don't know, exorcism? Analysis? You've gotta
understand, for a noisy month now the grackles
have been feeding on the crumbs of our quiddities.
Look: ants are still carting the morsels away
in long defiles.'
    'Nice work, if you can get it.'
    'And all the while I'm trying to put the pieces
back together and get on with it. But my reason
fails me, time and time again. You see, in logic
everything follows from a contradiction — and that
follows from its flip side, and is expressed in the rule
that *this cannot be allowed*,
which follows from everything.'
    'Ostensibler snake oil I've never —'
    'That's the hitch of course. A rule of discourse isn't
necessarily incumbent on the world at large — or the world
at small for that matter. Everything bears the possibility
of its opposite within itself, and would appear
utterly other by a single transposition of constituents.
Tragedy and Comedy, as Aristotle was wont to say,
are composed of the same letters.'
    'A rose by anagram would smell as *eros.*'

'Or sore.'
'Poem as mope.'
'Come again?'
'Not likely.'

'Between you and me, I have a feeling this longing
will be longer yet. Almost assuredly, yes. Extending and intending.
To the very penetralia of the chambered heart.'
    'To the very heart of longing, *kama-raga,*
one of the Three Poisons in the numerical
catalogue of the Mahayana:
from which all forms, space and time inter alia,
are shed as surd and remainder — salamanders and
nanoseconds, the involucre of an acorn, the emptiness
cupped in that involucre . . . certain opaque evenings
the color of eggplant, eggplants long and oblong,
pendulous as a Buddha's earlobes . . . debris on the breeze . . . .
And that khaki and camouflage form time puts on
when it's got enough wood to work with.'
    'I know: sycamore! But still, if the form of expression
isn't incumbent on the world, any reasonable relation
between our discourse and what it describes would have to be,
well, serendipity, or teleology. And I have issues with either.'
    'Then you ought to be equally wary of the alternative.
Put it this way: it's just as teleological to think that
the point of creation is to perplex you — *Chaos ab Ordine,*
flummox from cosmos. Whatever your theoretical misgivings
about the way language divvies up the world, in practice
you certainly take it at its word. And certainly
its distinctions come in handy: a hornet's nest
is not a piñata. Anyhow, whoever said logic's
supposed to *describe* anything? You've been sold
a load of goods. Mother of all snake oils —
liniment for the spasms of a phantom limb. Logic
is only in the interstices, in the bright space between words.'
    'Just as you used to be.'
    'Serendipity or teleology, it is a surely world suited
to your byzantine turn of mind, the kind given to
catenation of casuistry, with a jesuitical subtlety
and relish.'

'I don't know. We do things. We refrain from
doing things. Occasionally we feel sorry after.'
'The stirrings of a vestigial conscience, I detect.
Still, you must first learn the harsh teaching of *anicca*,
mujo, impermanence.'
'Got my *mujo* workin', baby, but it just don't work
on you.'
'And second, equanimity in the face of it —
an even keel against all odds. Most difficult
of things to master, and the most rewarding:
the gesture of rose in a vesture of thorns.
And this can only be nurtured through *bhavana*,
mental culture, balm and plaster for the
philophastering sore.
      All day the same our postures were,
      And we said nothing all day.'

'Seemingly,' and by jiminy if it doesn't feel
as if then and there all the ifs got unhitched
from their thens, 'Against which,
the atomies of which we grow?
And those legions of aeon?'
'The whiskers on a minute:
nothing there is that doesn't also seem.
And cannot be but in its place —
just as you used to say.'
'A koan, a conundrum —'
'The flight of one wing flapping: hey, why did Bodhidharma
cross the road?'
'Well all I know is that even this snippet
of interior dialogue's beginning to feel interminable.
And too arch. Too elliptical. And way too deranged
an exchange.'
'"Strain at a gnat and swallow a camel."'
'See? What the Sam Hill is that supposed to mean?'
'It means I have not yet begun to prate. So buckle up,
my hapless ambsace, my poet manqué, whilst I illustrate
the gist of it by way of an allegory of sorts. One in keeping
with the orientalizing theme here.
'Back in the declining, hidebound days of the Manchu
dynasty, many a mandarin kept track of the jaded hours

with the aid of an incense-clock: a slow-burning joss-coil
of successive essences ensconced within a maze-work
and hexagram-incised box; which allowed the odor-adroit
to tell the time of day by smell alone —
I shit you not: say, "Quarter past sandalwood,
time for my second pipe." Of course this is a
generic example, closing off from view more
than it reveals. Even still, in all the fantastical
cortege of timepiece oddities — egg glass, hour glass,
gnomon, clepsydra, atomic clock — was there ever
an instance to betray a solider sense of place
and duration inter-knit? It being the obverse of that
more familiar synthesis, the painted horizontal scroll:
such as, "Corteges and Trophy of the Tribute of the Kingdoms,"
whose craggy outcrops, ravines, precipices and abysses
hint at a sequential narrative — the hermitage,
the caravanserai, wave on volute wave as individual
as a brushstroke, bearing the junk flotilla, argosies
flush with pelf and tribute: heaped brocade,
huddled concubinage, bestiaries real and imaginary.
(Loplop down in the orlop
with cargo for the Emperor's new menagerie.)
The focal point of the whole scroll is of course the palace,
but even as you scrutinize, the scene deforms
imperceptibly, pattern takes shape. What were
but a moment ago desultory rivulets, mountain paths
intestine, are seen to be so many transforms on a same —
now the interstices of an immense pericarp,
itself only one third of the entire lotus
coming into focus, even as the palace
spontaneously recedes, revealing in sequent tableaux
dance stage, jewelled pond and dais. And what
minutely lapidary particulars!
Exquisite pearl-nets.
Moisty red eft!
Plasmagorical lights. Eftsoons
nebulous clusters of flower — and yet
you can discern each petal and on each
the eighty-four thousand veins. And the context
itself keeps on shifting as well, as you keep on losing
and finding yourself in all this — the eight charnel grounds,

the Circle of Gnosis — wait. I recognize this place:
Shambhala! Then that weren't no mundane Emperor —
that would have been the kalki, or lineage-king —
and the whole thing an inconceivable mandala-envisioning,
multi-storied, cubic, four hundred cubits in breadth, girded
by enceintes of the four elements and a high-voltage fence of vajras. So
then that inscrutable bandy-legged figure must be one of the
ninety-six satraps, but when he answers you with an
inscrutable beneficent beaming knowing smile wide enough
for the funambulist universe to traverse end to end
and back again, your heart doing saltimbanques to see
the teetering poise of galaxies slack-rope-walking —
you realize you had it all wrong: it's
Meeting with Amida under a tree!
And what trees: from the agate-colored blossoms
issue sapphire rays of light, from the sapphire-
colored blossoms, a green pearl light, never mind
the combinatorial explosion of coral, amber, jadeite, jacinth,
and the hundred Kotis of king-mani-gems. Plashing
about atop the jeweled sinkhole, mandarin drakes and their mates,
moorhens, gallinules and so forth, "all expounding
the wonderful Dharma. Whether in meditation or not,
you will always hear the wonderful Dharma" — I'm
quoting from the *Contemplation Sutra* . . . a long cry from
the Victor Segalin where we began. Finally, take note
of the Seven-jewelled Glorious Objects of the Land of Utmost Bliss,
and I hope I'm not giving *too* much away when I say
one among them is an exquisitely carved incense clock.'

    'Odd's bodikins! You know, not to come across as picayune
or such, but usually an allegory is *about* something. '
    'Well for one thing: notice how you never question
the *that* of it, even though the what keeps shifting beneath your sneakers.
You never say, "Hey wait a minute, I must be dreaming or tripping or
something." Beguiled by the mind-candy of it all I suspect.'
    'Maybe because it was all so vivid: so that your chinoiserie and your
Candyland description
seemed to have as much verity to it
as the waking workaday world.'
    'Or as *little*. Speaking of which have you noticed how
the more we talk the smaller we get?'

'I think it just seems that way,
'cause the poem is getting bigger.'
    'No, it's more of a Zeno type thing —
the minuter we go, the greater the hiatus
between us and the end.'
    'What about that incense clock?'
    'Merely a curious detail. But curiously apropos, wouldn't you say?'
    'Apropos of what?'
    'Because in the rock, paper, scissors of metaphysics,
smell trumps time — because of the immediate beeline, I'd say,
more than any other sense, between aroma and memory:
or haven't you noticed how some random whiff — kindergarten
paste! wet mittens! — cuts right across the years.
(Habituation is the tertium quid.) Are you aware there are
entire buddha-fields that accomplish the Dharma-work
wordlessly, by means of perfumes?'

To what end this abstracted yakety-yak I wonder, gazing out
across the Valleys of the Hundred Horseless Conjectures,
a green moony sky, and you know — I think we are shrinking.
And haven't even got to the gravamen yet.
Working against time. I should try and jump-start the conversation maybe.
(A slight shift of breeze or mind, bearing
the semantics of pine.)

'All of this has come to naught, I fear. Poem after poem
coming between us, less and less
candor in each. A terse *perdu perdu:*
thirty-two all told, all told in the tense of loss,
the aorist amorist. Would you agree?'
    'Truth be told, it is you who are speaking, not me.'
    'That would make me the fiction then. And then everything
I said — fictional?'
    'For the most part. But you know, universals are inherently flawed,
there's always an exception. Noah didn't need
to save the fish. Universally quantified propositions are universally false.'
    'If that proposition is true, then it is false.
(I mean, then at least one universal assertion is true —
that one.)'
    'But then if it's false also, again it would be true.'
    'And again false, and so and so forth . . . And what's to blame?

'Why language, Einstein, that allows you to invent me, and then invent
my absence, and insult to injury, then make me the mouthpiece
for your own absurd hypotheses.'
	'There is less calculation in this than you imagine.
At first there was a real girl, in a real tea hut . . .
Now it's gotten to the point that I never know what
you're gonna come out with.'
	'Well that makes two of us. Hey, I'm just providing a bit
of plot captioning here, to aid the figment-impaired.
These are not conclusions, just premises.'
	'To be sure. How many times have you loosed the dogs
to chase me off the conclusions . . . So,
whatever came of that Platonic half-an-ark?'
	'Still adrift I guess, on the metaphysico-parsimony:
they couldn't afford, you see, to give up the dove.'
	'In truth, I wish you'd stop beating about the ambush
and cut to the chase.'
	'Well here's the short and long of it —
first there's our sentiments: in a nutshell, gone.
And all the bygones also, gone beyond.'
	'And the hutness?'
	'Alas. Utterly gone beyond. Strangely enough,
that's just the grammar of place.'
	'It needs must be.'

So raise a rich tent for entity!
Fashion it particolor, and fix
the ridgepole to the polestar of plenty,
around which our emptiness revolves.
For even were you here any longer,
or had even you ever been,
you would've had have already withdrawn,
you'd have had had to go.
My quondam whilom sometime ambuscade.

Here's the situation then,
the long and short of it:
within the heart of an impossible lotus bud,
petal on folded petal of luminous script,
is hidden a Pure Land tea pavilion
constructed of words only —

sycamore beryl-ground nanosecond
miniscule agate-flower lopsidedness
nebulous flower clusters
Abode of the Unsymmetrical —
and there our absences sit
side by side
cross-legged, chain smoking,
making small talk.

[from the SPAT (Standard Poetical Aptitude Test)]

Part III (Metastases)

14. NUDIBRANCH is to CONIFER, as

(A)   flamingo : spirulina
(B)   merriment : motherlode
(C)   hairball : the fall of cherry blossoms at spring's end
(D)   *stanza my stone*

Part IV (Reading Comprehension)

Night unites us in incertitude.
I think. I'm none too sure anymore.
None of us is. We hope. Everybody
looking as askant as Kant at a
dogmatic slumber party. These looks
have hooks — like the cruel kitelines
children fly at dusk in Borneo
to snag the wings of fruit bats as they
leave the roost. And the oneiric flying fox.
Or maybe I'm projecting. I'm none
too sure anymore. None of us is.

These cafés are literally
littered with literati
nursing lattes.
(Exotic confections of organic
Mount Analogue arabica
and fresh quarts of camel's milk
flown in daily from a drome-dairy
in the Empty Quarter.)

21. In this passage the author illustrates
(A)   alliteration run amuck: after the dance, the restraining order
(B)   the typical and often dada misuse of the adverb "literally"
(C)   diction like an épée (long and fluted and coming to no point)
(D)   the modus ponens of caffeine buzz and over-the-top persiflage: verse as
        vice and vice versa

You can put a rhesus monkey in front of a mirror
and it just won't recognize its reflection. In fact
the monkey'll most likely attack the stranger it sees there,
even after living with that mirror for fifteen years. Humans
recognize their own features and so think themselves
superior. But put a man in front of a rhesus monkey
and he also fails to see himself, even after fifteen years
of solid research. In fact, we can live a hundred years or more
peering in the mirror of the world and yet somehow
never recognize ourselves therein.

22. According to the passage, the problem with rhesus monkeys is
(A)   a lack of cooperation with the scientific objectives of their keepers
(B)   poor self-image
(C)   a slight case of diaspora
(D)   sometimes you feel like a nut, sometimes you don't

A steady drizzle soaked us clean through to the marrow
as we sloshed past the Avante-Garde Cinema Mausoleum —
a brooding armory sort of edifice, routinely passed up by the city's
horde of moviegoers for the Googleplex Cinema on Houston.
I remember how we stopped for a spell by the little graveyard
where Preserved Fish waits out the lonely End Times
before continuing on our lonely little way to the bar on Ludlow
named for his descendent Max. From Hell-Gate to Battery everywhere
the sky was reflecting the ember eminence cast by the glowing ramparts of Dis.
In the impiety of the moment I tightened my hairshirt
and reached for your hand.

And I remember even now how
the pavement glistened here and there
where the streetlight sheds its sodium
and the rainbow sloughs its slick of skin
that stirred and steadied in
the steady almost imperceptible
rising and falling of 2nd Street
sleeping off its last meal.

23. The author implies that
(A)   fish may be preserved in a light wine sauce, or in brine
(B)   dreams everywhere are backing up onto the streets of our cities
(C)   the city is a moral battleground between the forces of alienation and piety

(D)   too much Dante can put a damper on a nice date

She's dictating her latest chanson de geste
her wording so cloying a steady
trickle of treacle runs down her chin
disappears into the Great Rift Valley
between her breasts and you know
she knows you can't stop trying
to follow it with your eyes, to follow
the flower of French nobility
down the treacherous pass to their
date with destiny. 'Alas! The Saracen
in your eyes, the symmetry
of your scimitar smile
are addling my impassive troubadour!'
'Please! This is my latest chanson de geste
that you are so interrupting. Be you
content for now with this.'
A perfumed veronica from her
cambric camisole and a million
flamingos erupt in your head
fling themselves into a cotton candy cloud
above a lake of caustic soda.
A lone jackal retreats,
trotting off with his lawn ornament.
And as you bow in gratitude
you imagine you can hear
the plaintive final note of Roland's horn
drifting out from the trouvère of her
haunted cleavage.

23. Which of the following statements is (are) supported by the passage?
I.   The early romances functioned much as the mental hygiene
        films of the 1950's, as a medium for teaching norms of social etiquette.
II.   The extremely alkaline nature of those lakes makes them
        toxic to all but the flamingo and the spirulina it feeds on.
III.   Ask not for whom the telephone rings. "It's for thee."

(A)   I only
(B)   II only
(C)   I and II only
(D)   I and III only

Song

I'm an infertile delta.
You're the inundating Nile.
I'm the abandoned barnacle.
You're the new moon tide.
I'm the incredible Henry Limpet
crying L-a-a-dy Fish! L-a-a-a-dy Fish! —
and then the plaintive sonic thrum.
You're of course the fish I'm thrumming for.

I'm hawk's cry in a dry season.
You're the water table.
Every time the dowser skirts your house
that hazel switch is twitching in his hands.

I'm a caravan of humped ideas:
these above all else have been
the lumbering dromedaries
of my waste years.
And there on the horizon your eyes —
a mirrored mirage
double oases
twin cisterns at whose profound
no book no bucket
no stone no plummet dropped
did ever sound —
sister wells
where the barefoot muses themselves
come sometimes to draw a jarful
and depart.

Your head lies on the pillow
looking up, your eyes
brimful of the sky.
I'm the willow leaning over,
leafless, tensile, suffering
the elements, searching out.
And with my straining taproot now
I touch the source.

Hail the Conquering Gypsy Moth

Shape-shifter   All-devourer
Denuder of Nations —

Saplings are happening
in the mind of spring,
heady the pheromones
perfuming the breeze,
and already a fine white death
is spun in a crotch of branches.

Hail the sovereign gypsy moth
Supreme Assimilator —
from stone garden in ole Kyoto,
from wooded love-den of the brooding Bulgar,
they have hung up gnosis
traded satori for the
far subtler doctrine of Manifest Destiny.

Every single gypsy moth is terrible!
Thus a monograph I have prepared,
"Of the terrible green ichor that swells unbeknownst
in our midst, being an examination of the
'Gypsy Moth' phenomenon, *Lymantria dispar* or *Porthetria
dispar*, and incorporating an elucidation of their harsh
and otherwise antinomial teaching,"
endeavors to combat our relative nescience of the subject
with Science (that is, in the larger sense of *Wissenschaft*),
to this end running through, however cursorially,
the wider themes implicated in the career
and life history of this species:

1.)   The egg. As idea,
          as yet void of content, at the same time
          perennially explaining and explained by
          the formal power of our thinking, pullulating, etc.
          (I think about a whole people
          who reckoned by a purpose
          made manifest, a nation with a Destiny.

A Destination.
And how it all fell apart when they got there.
Did they get there?)

2.)   Love as larval craving
(or alternately, the vehicle of grace).

3.)   The invisible worm from tree to tree
shall weave New England's winding sheet.

4.)   As all mortal things —
    by flimsiest filament hung
squirming, suspended on
    nothing, embroidered
and bejeweled,
    a sack of marmalade.

5.)   For however many PBS documentaries
you've clocked in on, and whatever the
number of sheepskins tacked to your wall, how well
can you tell reality from bullshit? Were I to inform
you there's an ant that sports pincer-like mandibles
half again the length of its whole body, which when
opened wide gape a full 180 degrees (long and
elegant they are, like Dalí's unfurled mustachios),
and which when snapped shut (clocked at a third
of a millisecond — the fastest movement hands down
of anything yet recorded in the animal kingdom)
will catapult said insect two or three feet into the air,
somersaulting onto the person of any approaching
myrmecologist, over whom she and her myrmidon
confederates will formicate and painfully sting;
and if I further avowed that formication is not a
venial sin, but a swarming of pismires, and that
"pismire" is just another word for ant (Middle
English *pisse-myre*, "from the urinous smell
of an anthill"), would you buy it, or any part of it,
or would you ask to see my poetic license and/or
animadvert on this recent and irresponsible penchant
for Dada in the world of letters?

6.) The gypsy moth was first worshipped in Second Dynasty
Egypt, where metamorphosis ("Swaddling out of
[its] own gut [disjecta membra]") inspired new and fascinating
approaches to necrolotry.

> *It is Re who first called forth the names*
> *from out of his own members [Ka].*
> *Wherefore do we canopically*
> *in one unbroken silken soliloquy.*
> (*Pyramid papyri,* Fr. 1170a)

7.) Q. How do you make a pheromone?
A. Kick him in the mummy.

8.) When you suggested we catch the matinee
as it was munching politely in the sargassum fronds,
I confess I was at a loss and hence my green
ictus. But I digress.

9.) Q. How is Destiny like the gypsies of Lorca's
Boda de Sangre?
A. They both play at "cast-a-net."

10.) Egg again.

11.) Entering the City with Bliss-bestowing Hands.

Perhaps, after all, you meant manatee?

Saplings are happening
in the mind of spring,
heady the pheromones
perfuming the breeze,
and desire is a fine white death
dozing in a crotch of branches, etc.

Fit the Third

Ogygian Journal

1

Sitting on a rotting dock
propped on a scrap of river —
fished-out, backwashed
and lapsed back to rust
— time's native hue — where
everything just stops,
where even the rushes cease rushing
and the fiddlers waving oversized claws
and the orb weavers weaving orbs
et cetera et cetera
and a sort of peaceable abeyance
a palpable sort of buoyancy
permeates this place
for the space of two or three breathings,
as the tide turns

and a ragged heron, ashen-cast,
like the shadow of a doubt
ushers in dusk, prolegomenon
to that uncertainty where all shadows meet —
and comes at last, if not the bright awaited insight
or some burning resolve, at least
a modicum of equanimity:
and what fascinating patterns my anxiety makes
cast on the mind's panorama —
fractious, exactly like the rippling
reflected on that listing hull,
or almost — a kind of sinking
that makes it sway, "drawing water,"
and where the keel intersects, the fluid
modulating line breaks off
into a mevlevi of eddying centers,
as elsewhere

the crabs shuttle and evade like metaphors,
that is, sidewise,
and everything purposes to its proper refuge,

the kestrel on its stump of palm,
the mind in its thicket of consequences,
(and all these contradictories
buzzing around like deerflies) —
as darkness a carapace comes on
a pace apace
comes on as common integument
to our peculiar qualms.
Is there any unravelling of it all?

(I'm a frayed knot.)
Is there no end to the unravelling?
Can't begin to say I say aloud.

Back in the banked world,
on the one hand bracken and mangrove
on the other hand bracken and mangrove,
and between — the rank ineluctable
of-coursing through, a kind of thinking
that makes its way, silted, fish-lit,
brackish as it may be.

                2
I swear I've seen the craziest things here —
a smack of jellyfish big as a cadillac
perambulating,
reef squid shootin' the shit
by way of fluent tattoo,
startled garfish go skittering
upright over the water on their tailfins
like so many Charlie Chaplins in fast-forward.
Some things I just don't get —
that sign by the roadway for one,
SLOW, POLICE SLEEPING —
the pidgin of patois for another —
and some I'm not sure I want to,
like the Jah Elvis Cultural Center
up in the hills.

First time was in '91, we checked in,
my brother and I, the day they started Desert Storm.

Solitudinem faciunt, tempestatem apellant.
In the journal wrote, "Find myself with
several planeloads of compatriots
here to loosen our moral belts a notch or two,
while halfway 'round the globe we are visiting on Baghdad
our ten kiloton categorical imperatives.
Every half-hour everyone crowding by the bar
to watch the show on CNN, sorties
elbowed out by Minivans, Happy Meals, designer perfumes,
then back to a stack of B-52's 'in a formation
called stairway to the stars,' like mechanical paraclete
of the lost creation. Three F-15's whine by
dopplering up and down the scale of the insane,
cockpit shots of pinpoint pac-man accuracy,
eerie light of night video, tracer fire and flak
crisscrossing a green Mesopotamian sky.

"Then on to the pep rally, Anytown,
baton tipsy
                    rayon hot pants majorette
leading on a hook-and-ladder triumph car,
the kindled id flickering between Iraq and a hard place.
Faces bathed in cathode ray, happy on
beer weed fuzzy navels daiquiris (overproof)
and some conflagrating parti-colored concoction
they like to call a 'flaming fuck'
that comes back up as quickly as
down it went . . ."

O.K. Indulgently put. But in some instances,
proleptically as well:
". . . because I know much oil will be spilled,
and much blood spilled over it,
and the slick of it spreads dumbly over my thinking . . .
Just now some small talk poolside, a paisano sizing me up
between chapters of his Turow — second question inevitably,
what do you do? When I want to cut it short I tell the truth.
Then there's always pronouncing on the 'ugly American'
it goes without saying though it always gets said,
a commonplace of the genre, even expected, as if the set it singled out —
the tourist class — membered everybody but the author. But

somehow being at war I can see myself more clearly in these,
and as others see us: half-baked, half-witted,
guileless dupes, fungible individualists, righteous, self-righteous,
self-besot, dislocated, attention deficit, anywhere, everywhere
but here, loudmouth, fanfaronading, paranoid, patronizing,
fatuous, fat-cat, fat, Homeric (as in Simpson), wearing our
hearts on our t-shirts (everybody's with Stupid). Somehow
being at war makes the hypocrisy of our innocuous-enough
posturing stand out in relief. More specific? How about
this self-righteous pretense that it's about one nation infringing
on the sovereignty of another. Can anyone say 'Panama'?
I mean it was only a year or so ago. Forget politics. How about —
ridiculing Rastafarians for their outlandish belief system,
while continuing to construe holy writ as a sort of Resurrection
habeas corpus? Creed as a Get-Out-of-Hell-Free card.
(And Rasta say, 'Ironic you be so righteous fightin' wit I-raq,
when it just de new Babylon pummelin' on de old.')
You know they ran that damn commercial long enough —
'Our distractions come in all shapes and sizes, one for every
occasion' — in all its fungible brands from infancy on up
until finally we bought it — the body: the ever-improvable,
improbable body, now on display in all its corpulent-opulent
lipo-sucked, collagen-plumped glory-be-to-body ugly truth,
buoyed up and down the shore here by vanity's
implanted flotation devices."

Seven-odd years later
the identical shit hitting the familiar fan.

Back at the hotel concatenation hath made its masterpiece:
Stubs of ganj' crushed butts of Craven A's
soak in ashstrewn estuaries disgorged
from rolling Redstripe bottles where flies
disport themselves, as upended highballs
fêted with swizzles and exotic cocktail parasols
announce the departed happy hour.
Lolling in an imperious martini glass
a glass eye surveys the waste
ozymandiously.

3

As darkness a carapace comes on
and the root man limps home
and the duppy creeps out
from a worried knot in the cotton tree
and somewhere you can hazard
a shandy bottle is being buried at a crossroads
and hurriedly, then
quite suddenly for a spell
gradually all at once
the land erupts
abruptly by degrees
in chorusing huzzahs
and hosannas
avian kyries
amphibian eleison
the entire syllabary of clarion
insisting *it is here*
         the cricket's thin timbrel
iterating *it is now*
         the katydid recitative
and drifting out over the whole island:
treefrogs — piping
tumultitudinously — these
that the Phrygians knew
as the "shrill-voiced Hesperides."
It is a complicated sound
a recombinant sort of sound
the sound of a mind
digit by digit
being pried loose of its grip —
just the prevailing vernacular
the algorithm of the commonplace
gone all out of bounds,
drowning by degrees the dogs
ringing the horizon and even
the mnemonic pam-pam
of the ever-liminal sub-woofers.

And now the mind unmooring
starting to drift out on it
is *called back*
by a croak out of pre-history
and *holy shit — right there*
great-grandmother heron
hunched on her creaking stilts
stares back at me from the primordial shallows.
Her eye a cross-hairs.
Her brain a trip-wire.
My every step's a trespass,
hers a calibration.
Again that frilled squawk
the color of grave dirt and ashes,
as from a trance-fixity her strung neck
oscillating at the fundamental
distracts the cocking of her gait,
at first a slight displacement of the nothing,
but to the crone-adapted eye
a stance whose gist is *chance* and *mystery.*
She is eldest of the gods.
She is Obeah,
and this is her balmyard.
And the name of this place
on the maps
is the Great Morass.

4

One of those Grand Meaulnesian days
when anything can happen and usually does,
I set out into the arbitrary analogies
past the rasta shack its red green yellow
painted slats, through the cassava patch
and bean patch
eked out of the ooze,
threading the thin margin
between river and morass,

sun's hammer on brain's anvil,
the wind whipping a pantomime from the plants,

or actually, caricatures of plants — jackfruit,
breadfruit, giant fern — huge-leafed things
nodding un-huh un-huh or just
gesticulating in ambivalence
an indolence of apprehensiveness
whatever that really means
in all features great and small,
down to the tiny-leafed "shame lady"
(watch your step) a sensitive mimosa
who folds them up at the first caress,
but, who can say, lingeringly? A swoon? Or with
deliberation, much the way a girl named Pearl
folded up the valentine
and sent the resulting Concorde of my hopes
into a tailspin
over the sixth grade homeroom.
Wait — sensitive and animate? Ha!
The pattern is more porous than the categories let,
more skillfully plied
Deus sive Natura (incidentally, equivalent in gematria)
and who'd ever guess,
so seamless is the seeming of it all.

Reflect if you will on the dance of the banana
spiders as they synthesize intricate fastenings,
flawless tautologies — the "Anansi Rope" —
down among the thatch of woven reeds. I've often wondered,
how is it the wee little mandala weavers
never seem to catch themselves? Here's
a clue: in all such webs the radials, the first laid,
are unglued, tramlines and trestle to the lattice they sustain,
and on it the renowned ambidextrous
artist inlayed a dance
such as once in broad Knossos
Daedalos crafted for Ariadne
of the lovely hair —
always mending a gape, tending the wound of an old struggle,
or complexifying the pattern
with nimble half-turns and side-stepping,
like a planet backpedalling in epicycles,
that nonetheless makes its way

in decaying orbits to the hub —
an architectonic of interstices, a stitch in time,
a certain recursiveness, wheels within wheels
but seeded with the erratic the absurd
so as not to give the game away too soon,
and who'd ever guess, so seemless
is the seaming of it all.
Now sift the universe through, field what it can.

Up ahead, furthering me into
shade and shape of foliage blent,
a cocky mockingbird runs through all its
stratagems, no theme, just variations —
or is this yet another variation would
it were not so on the ever-elusive self-same
we keep stumbling into here, the very theme
of themes and scheme of schemes, the
design of all design,
to wit: the Will to Illusion?
Look about, the fulsom of assent.

A pair of parrots chatterbox from tree to tree,
a couple of four-flushers, flashing their money
wherever they go. Up in that ackee branch —
a thimble-sized nest cupping a thumb-sized
hummingbird, snug in its torpor.
(Look closer, it zips away.)
Jesu, it could go on like this forever.
Prickly scrub amock blossoming in expletive.
In the center a clearing is made
and unmade by my stumbling into as
the ambient leaves lift from their stems,
transmogrify to *Heliconius charitonius*,
the zebra longwing butterfly. These are shy flyers,
five or six looping slow ellipses
around each other, kept aloft by the faintest vibration
of their elongated wings, black and yellow banded,
the design of whose design when seen in flight
is this: to beguile the mind.
Heaped around
in a circle of enchantment
bleach the bones of would-be predators and lepidopterists.

dauncerly and more, o mariposa

And a voice, about as quiet
as your usual musings, but insistenter,
sinuating, 'the *temenos, remember?*
The glade from way back when where
you would someday make your way,
have you forgot? Is this not such a place?
And is it not all too late?'

And the wind,
blowing
from some unweeded
hortus conclusus
of memory,
concurs.

dauncerly and more, o mariposa

Back at the hotel, The Last Resort,
middle of the night, eerie laughing:
two rooms over the vacationing physicist
and sometime Platonist — one of the
form-tormented school,
dreams a fifth force, quintessence,
counterposed to gravity —
levity, the final equation and philosopher's
anti-stone.

　　　5
The sea, the sky's beloved handmaiden,
wrung from the sky, scouring a coral outcrop.

The air carries the tang of serenity.
The tongue pronounces it "salinity."

Breathe in, the waves probing for every crevice,
an anemone of fingers.
Breathe out, attenuating in counter-thrust
to a cerassee, a vineyard of tendrils.

Sundown, and the whole limpid scene
the whole planet it would seem
is layered in the no-color sheen that is
immaculate nacre
slimed over this bit of grit
a nuisance, a minute irritation
caught in vacant space — no make that
caught in the lustre of abyss . . .
(Sounds pellucider.)

How carefully then the sea, sky's beleaguered consort,
broadens the design
stitching it with gold thread
and simultaneously unlooming it.
Her suitors never do catch on.
It could ostensibly go on like this forever
when without warning the same dissolves
into the particle-pageant. (I don't know
if you've ever seen this) like television snow —
starting at the vanishing point
and sweeping out,
            the atomic swerve
incorporates everything before it
before it resolves back into waves again.
In this manner it vacillates and the mind likewise
ambiguates before it.

'And,' the physicist is quick to interject,
'you can never step into the same ocean twice,
or both at the same time, or either the one or the other
before measurement, that is. Know what I mean?'
Well frankly I don't, and neither does he, I'll wager,
so I off him with a bit of diatribe:

'These days there is nothing so absurd
but some physicist has said it. You know I can't help but
notice an irony at work here. More than anything else
it was your success at empirical discipline and theoretic
rigor that spelled the demise of speculative
thinking. But who today is responsible for the oddest
excesses of speculation? It's as if

at the end of all that rigor significance has to sneak in
through the back door. And finally your interpretive
gestures prove to be as arbitrary as anyone else's.
The difficulty's not that it can't be done, but that it
can be done in any way you please. And then, Holy Moses,
it runs the full spectrum. From the *esse est percipi*
of the empirical orthodoxy, vamping it in idealist drag,
to the Hegelian outright of those Final Anthropics,
who project some future über-consciousness thinking
us all into existence. A captivating tableau:
31 different flavors, yum yum: gnostic limbos
of multiverse; the Hwa Yen of "quantum principles"
implicating the whole in every morsel, and wedded
to demure variables that must, by the uncertainty purdah,
remain veiled and unseen — and then of course
the Zen of Copenhagen: no models of ultimate
reality possible — equanimity in the face of paradox, mixed
with a dollop of Wittgenstein (you know, "whereof one
cannot speak . . ."). All the term-hampered attempts
at describing what you call a superposition: here there
yes and no and both and neither, and the cross product
of them all — hey, that's *madhyamika*-speak — nothing
new in trying to frame original nature. Then Protagoras
steps in with a measurement and presto: collapse of the wave
function (Ψ). The ineffable hooked on Poseidon's trident.
So there poses today's great matter of mind: a particle
waving. A mite of a thing that pops up like a rabbit out of a hat,
the outcome of some mathematical legerdemain. Or else
if you can't buy that, a modulation of the inexhaustible,
a sort of stinginess of a kind of profligacy, like
Beethoven counting out his coffee beans, in any case
a double entendre that nobody catches, or better yet,
a sloppy poet mixing his metaphors.'

'And don't forget Schrödinger's hapless cat, while you're
at it, who on the received account backs us all into
our separate solipsisms: the packet collapses, the cat is gassed —
or isn't — and reality is made determinate for each observer per se
(and observer of observer, etc . . .). You think we're
comfortable with that?'

'I imagine not. 'Cause in the end two tenets from
Aristotle resurface: that substance is essentially
identical with its intelligible constitution, and that
matter is, with regard to itself, unknowable.
And that must be tough, to have to pin it all
on the mind's intrusion.'

'It's like balancing the world on the back of a turtle.'

'But then you guys have always wheeled out
the intellect, *ex machina*, whenever you needed to give
a direction to time.'

'No, we've got non-linear functions and irreversible processes
(coming out of thermodynamics) that can do that now. See you can't
say where things are going anymore without infinite precision
on the initials. And so you can't run the equations backwards
either.'

'*You* can't. We ought to be more careful with our terms.
Like "determined" and "determinate." Or "indeterminate"
and "limited predictability." You know infinite precision
is not a priori beyond the ken of an
infinite intellect. But even if no one
knows where it's going, its course could
still be determinate. Of course, as an exercise
in homiletics — I mean as a sort of skeptical *caveat,*
what you're saying is fine. Although we'd gotten to
this point before — before, that is, ole Immanuel ex-
humed the fresh corpse of causality, and breathed a
seeming life into its nostrils. *State contenti,*
umana gente, al quia . . . But then of course we're
only looking at one kind of causality, efficient
cause, the chain link of effects stretching across time.
Formal causes, for instance, are quite beyond your
imaginings.'

'Perhaps that's because it is a beyond and an imagining.'

'Probably. It relies on a picture, no doubt. But so do
all these conceptual fables. I don't see how

you can do without pictures, and anyway I like
mine better than yours.'

'And do pray tell what's that?'

'Conceive, if you care to, the proceedings before us,
the big picture, *sub specie causae formalis* — not
opposed to or even instead of the efficient
conditions; but rather, orthogonal to, and cutting across
the temporal axis, this:
concentricities on concentricities of power
surmounting by degrees,
every degree container and contained,
each a self-organizing, self-maintaining *conatus*
as formal microcosm and expression of single substance.
(That is, to each thing its measure of independence,
if you will, *imitatio dei*. That is, in the face of all else, namely,
the web of interdependency.) It is this alone
that distinguishes measure from measured, and
this that incorporates others into its measure
(a ruler measured is just a piece of wood.)'

'So mind is implicated after all.'

'Yes, so long as "being used as — " or "self-maintaining"
are granted as mental attributes — and then it's turtles
all the way down.'

'Yertling into the abyss.'

'*Conatus*, remember, is marked by a "characteristic
relation" — not the individual elements, which are
always in exchange anyhow. That's the difference
with classical atomism. And that's the sinew
you have to reach for when wrestling with this concept.'

In the beginning was the formula . . .

And now and forever
the ever-penultimate equation
is scribed on the shore's tabula:

from out of its own element
in unnumbered solvent ciphers
scribbled and just as soon erased,
palimpsestuously.

The sea, the fugitive queen!
She that carries the moon in train —
herself in other guise — with
equal and opposing force.
Whose regnant geometries infiltrate
far up the tidal flats.
It is she arrays the gods
in all their estuarial gimmickry,
a glittering chain of beings,
from gnat totems in spouts of fluxion
to the long-legged bird-like things
stalking the alluvial plains.
She it is and no other
that plots the subtle slope of the ibis' throat
the mangrove its flying buttresses,
that loads the date palm
braided with sweet longing,
and raises up the royal palm
from out of the house of Judah,
towering above the court intrigues,
whose skin is redolent of balm and primogeniture,
whose skin is lofty with it, indeed,
whose lichen-mottled skin smells so exactly
like my grandmother's.

'Tell me, what's the chance that those things up there
are pterodactyls?'

'Shiver me timbers — frigate birds!'
Fregata magnificens
who with deva-like aloof
all but disdain to touch the earth —
only to fledge their young really —
scudding off now perasperadastra
(through the spars to the stars . . .).

6   A small parable

Q.   How do you shew the bottle fly the way out of the fly-bottle?
A.   There, it is out!

The first crepuscular glimmerings of dawn.
I was just sitting down to write this part of the opuscule
when I noticed an ant crawling on my arm. I should add that
this ant looked to have gone astray. That is to say, she
didn't appear to be on a scouting mission, or on the war
path or on any path at all, having lost it was plain to see
all trace of the chemical trail to the way back home. Like
when the crow in the folk tale ate up all the breadcrumbs. So
here's this pitiful bitty Gretel of a thing, sans crumb-
trail, sans Hansel, wandering the Black Forest where
admittedly one follicle looks pretty much like another.
Who wouldn't have taken pity? It's like I always say, our good deeds depart us,
they drop like ripe apples, while the bad sour on the branch
that grew them. If you run with the wolves,
you can't lie with the sheep.
(This proverb came to me in my sleep.)

Of course, now that you mention it, I suspect it's true, that in older variants
the crow must have played a more substantial role: you know,
the trickster who works to subvert our conscious ingenuities.
The best laid plans of ants and men . . . . But more importantly,
he tells us *to get lost*.
Sometimes the only way across the Great River
is to *step over*. (I forget, is the crow in the employ of the witch?)

So, getting back to it, I next
took the trouble to construct
this *ant-sized ladder*
for her to scale, because ants
are people too, you know,
I mean, everybody's a somebody.
But when I came back
lo and behold she was gone. Sometimes,
I said to myself, the best way out of the Dark Wood is to just
drop off.

The anoles are in amorous display today
and the gnats, still at it. Their frantic
rustic atom dance.

7
Thus
have I heard.
The universe is
actually Buddha-
shaped: peering
from the topknot
of the present
moment down the portly
mild rotundity of it all back
to the big bang its antipodes
(just as in Dante's Empyrean,
the point *compassing* its girth)
the "retroverse," so-called, ap-
pears from any point of view to
be a buddhiform hypersphere, or
rather, hyper-pear, mottled with light
("in yonder heaven the *lumen gloriae*")
ripening on a branch in Samarkand or
elsewhere
.

8
'Now yer crabs are barbarians, plain 'n simple.
For one thing, look at their language.
For another — they *eat* their *own*:
crab a la mode!
Down in crabtown
anything goes . . .
Their shanties are jest a hole in the ground!
'Course they're proud a them jes the same,
sit at the door they do an' wave ya by,
an' ev'ry now 'n then I gotta admit I find myself there —
jes' ta chuck the mumbly peg, y'know,
an' roll the round rum lingo. (A rule a thumb:

bring plenty a bandages.) And once [hushed now]
I witnessed *the bizarre goin's on* a their *nuptials.*
A crab wedding! The bride wore "pink" —
I mean ta say, she hadn't no shell on, seriously,
naked as a tattooed polynesian on shore-leave.
Hadda ask a hermit ta pinch me, y'know,
ta see if I was dreamin'.
Anyhow the jimmy does this ritual thing their males do,
flexin' his big claw in a sidewise sorta salute,
like this —
while the fiddlers performed a delicate an' I must say
disarmin' minuet. So comes time he shuttles the she-crab off
to his nuptial bower in the riverbed (by the way,
once a she-crab's wed they calls her a *sook*). Anyhow
as I was sayin', the fiddlers kept things goin' pretty neat,
a regular trenchtown chivaree — till aroun' midnight when —
get this — ever'body begins a-wavin their pincers in a unison
up at the moon.
Now I seen some strange customs in my day —
but when that great cracker-claw-in-the-moon
waved back —
boy I tell you, my eyes nearly
popped offa their stalks!'

       9
There is no word for it really, for the way
some things manage to stay put
by moving in every direction at once —
the ocean in its susurration of surround,
the Great Crab Nebula,
the unencumbered mind —
so I'm going to attempt one:
      lodgitation.

Bit too . . . I don't know. Textbookish.
("The universe and its generations
maintain a foothold by continually lodgitating.")
Or
      sparagmosis.

Better. Pedantic still, more so, but it's got
the pull and push of large masses,
and the pipe dream of equilibrium, and I like
the way it could be stretched to connect, say,
cell division with the fate of the child Zagreus.

In the Orphic cosmogony, we, the race of mortal schleps,
are born in the wake of that monstrous crime, perpetrated
by the gypsum-plastered *titanoi*. As with the Kabbalists
later, all matter — "frozen energy" in the modern trope —
is deemed to bear a spark of the sundered god.
And we who move and have our separate being
as by abscission from the absolute —
our brief is but to find and mend (re-
member) it.

No, I don't believe in collective guilt, really.
But I do believe in collective skeleton.
Take coral for instance:
star coral, of all sorts and magnitudes,
fire coral, in several brands,
fan, elkhorn and
brain coral,
          so-called because
like everything else
          it thinks! Enthralling, truly,
the labyrinthine catacombs of gyri and sulci.
Have you seen those haunting sad dwellings
built entirely of mastodon bones
(from our salad days on the Siberian savanna)?
Imagine then a Rome as a sort of reverse ossuary,
erected from the carcasses of her
slaves and caesars. But we the exiled
who are shed as surd and detritus,
what do we know of the ancestors,
living peremptory in our own bones
instead of theirs?
Our stance, however firmly planted,
is rootless as the sea herself. And even she
our first mother
is as a cipher to us.

The devoid of her quatrain, o!
the deuteronomy of her ocarina!
the bastinado of her coloratura!
Go ahead I defy you
try and pry a gist from it. Or
look askance at the bounding main,
a man-stance, arms akimbo.
Poke at it with a stick.
Go down to the sea in ships
or put it up to your ear.
You can hear —
the inside of a conch shell!
Keep a sea vigil
and strain to make it out
the tripping patois —
but all the words are jumbled together
every proposition and its opposite
canceling one another in an expanding pleonasm.

The sea has too much to say!
Every breaker rushing to judgment . . . .

Yes I confess to all this, like how many before,
guilty of it in how many guises — prowling on
the jutting prow of a headland half
outta your gourd and howling back at it
whitmaniacal, or sandymount-stranded
dreaming by the shore, a crescent moon
pasted to your pale forehead.
Or posing an idea of order beyond the mens of mar —
but what human solipsism could withstand
that comprehension?

There is a place I know
where the sea is always in a wroth
and limbs of coral
and torsos and
hand-over-handfuls of it
bleached to the bone of moon
lie tossed along the shore in gibbous knobs,

as if there were a demiurge
and this were his garbage heap,
and as if the discarded forms were
stranger and more perfect
than any finished workmanship.
A teeming vacancy, a trove
of archetype-encrusted failings:

organ-pipe coral
        blowing magnum mysteriums,
        fugues and enigmadrigals,
well-tempered coral,
what-not coral,
I dream of coral Jeannie,
figment coral, coral
of simulacrum.
Here is where I learned the very same of form and emptiness.

I say to any of you if any there be
who perched on a promontory or
marooned at the world's rim
has looked on the lens of the sky
through the spectacles of Spinoza,
who likewise find yourself in such a place
as this, amid the rubble of an immensity —
go ahead — pick up a poor yorick of it,
stare into the empty sockets of coral.

10

Seven-odd years here off and on
marooned, "pellbound,"
in thralldom to the softly-braided nymph
(renowned the island over as the River Maid, she is
feared as a powerful duppy and undine). Rarely seen,
but often felt: and more often smelt — her presence
redolent of must of grape and knotty pine
and a heady scent like damask stained with wine.
And Night jessamin, which the Spanish call
"damas de noche," but whose secret name
is *The Stars' Disequilibrium*. She makes

her home in a cave near the Blue Hole,
and there stirs her pepperpot of
bloodfeathersparrotsbeakdogteethtoothofcrocodile
bottleglassgravedirtrumandeggshell
the whole olla podrida and vile farrago of evil.
And there also keeps her gallipots, vials, thumb-stoppered ampoules with
their curious labels,
"oil a tun back," "oil a carry-away," "oil a keep-im-down,"
"oil a bamba," "dead-man's drops."
The entrance is well-hid by all manner of trees:
breadfruit, pendulous with it, vine entwined.
Mimosa, where the angels hang their wings to dry.
Gumbolimbo, poinciana, spadothea: or Flame of the forest,
its ember-orange
flowers holding up
the cupped remnant
of last night's rain.
Fig leaves covering their own nakedness.
Likewise an ackee tree, roots splayed, limbs akimbo,
a dance instructor's stance.
And on a whole other level —
the cotton tree, Lord of Dancers,
swaying from topknot to taproot
in the cycles of creation / destruction,
one limb rattling the pod of generation,
an extremity charred with the thunderstruck
of unction, a root planted firmly on the back
(ouch!) of nescience.
One limb raised in the fear-not gesture.
At its base shelter 'duppy umbrellas," as this most-prized
of mushrooms is called, while a spring
bubbling up nearby takes its channels here and there
where the water winds and plaits the parsley and the watercress,
her hair and only dress.
She picks no violet.
The violets pick her to be beholder.

Even a god coming upon this place
would gaze and feel his heart beat with delight,
as one now did —
Hermes! in his fleetest form:

the "doctor bird,"
a hummingbird of jet
whose beak is as of agate,
whose breast is encrusted
emerald,
whose tail is twin streamers
twining in languor —
that is the garland
of an agility — and
with which he mazes the eyes
of those mortals he would maze.

Long time the Wayfinder was in parley with the Mistress of the Isle,
while she set before him a table of the god-sustaining
Green Ginger Wine and the ambrosial Number Eleven mango:
and when they emerged I was over by the balmyard,
          under a canopy of immortelles
singing to myself, where for accompaniment
vermilion hibiscus blare like sousa trombone —
where now he stoops to nectar, pauses
                                        and is gone.

'. . . *One bright mornin' when my work is over, gonna fly away home.*'

'You can stop pining and start packing. That was your reprieve.'

'*No chains around my feet, but I'm not free.*
I know I am bound here, in captivity.'

'Hapless mortal — listen, the gig is up. Enchantment time is over; you can go
home now. Why not deploy that free will you mortals are always boasting
about?'

'I've been entertaining the hypothesis that crustaceans aren't terrestrial in
origin. Them crabs in all probability are probes. From Mars. Hear that
clicking? Radio telemetry. I've been picking it up in my fillings. Probably it's
pictures they're transmitting, maritime and riverine video — fluvial souvenirs.
Their own aquifers and canals having long gone dry, you know . . . So you're
tellin' me I have my free will again: after all these years wonderin' who put the
hoodoo on me and why . . . and I'm supposed to buy it?'

'Not exactly. I give you back the miraculous illusion of free will. Enjoy.
If you give yourself over to it, it can be quite exhilarating.
Like a joyride on the handlebars of a dilemma.'

'Sorry. Not interested in any more illusions. I want the real thing.'

'Hon, I hate to be the one to have to tell you, but
I'm afraid they ain't no "real thing." In fact, come to think of it,
free will is about the most moronic oxymoron you mortals have yet
to devise — after "free market," that is. A stubborn presumptive
and mental Monroe Doctrine. Down here we call it
"free necessity." Even a mortal can see there's no intrinsic
relation between will and its object. Remember Krishna's
injuction to Arjuna: you have the right to action, but
not to the fruits of action. Acting without attachment
to the fruits — that is the heart of Gita.'

'Fine. No problem, mon. Maybe I can live without final causes.
And yes, maybe intention even is on the threshold
of an ignorance. But tell the truth it's like I just keep on
going in circles. An error for every trial (and a trial for
every error (and a hanging judge for every hung jury (and three
Eumenides for every fury (in truth it'd take a Titantic
to stow all the mistakes I've made)))) . . .'

'And a waiting floe for every maiden voyage.'

'I remember I had this dream once, I was on some kind of field trip
with my Ontology class. We were wandering around
this trackless waste talking philosophy. All of a sudden
we come across these mysterious footprints in the mud.
We knew we were supposed to follow them, and so we did,
talking philosophy all the time. After a long while
somebody realized that the footprints were our own.'
(Mercury rising, slowly we retired to her cave, conversing all the while.)

'In truth it doesn't matter how you proceed. Some beings
learn best through endless cycles of remorse, contrition
and redemption. Well and fine. But isn't it possible at least
that free will is a willed illusion? That you *desire*
to be solely responsible for your actions, and even cling

to it? And that this desire is itself selfish, like all illusions
of control? The source of action is obscure. No human
knows its beginnings. No god but Necessity.'

'That's the old question — whether Necessity is really incumbent on the world at
large — or the world at small for that matter: electrons, pi-mesons, top-heavy
quarks seem to follow their own quirky laws. And everything built of them
inherits that fuzziness. A single amino can make the difference between two
people — or even between ways of seeing red.'

'But I tell you even there she will have her say: Fata Margana
in her island realm of La Nova. Tell that to the phosphorescent Nile strand.'

'Hold on, I'm almosting it . . ."transcendent philosophers."'
(This was just our way of gabbing sometimes. Somewhere between *gloze* and *glossolalia*.
More between "glossolalia": an ambivalent term, meaning the "gift of tongues" or
the psychobabble of schizophrenics. Funny, because the word's schizophrenic —
and us, negotiating the tightrope, the high tension wires betwixt.)

'This is the difference between gods and mortals: you resist/obey Necessity.
We *dance* with her.'

(At the warm center an ingot of foxfire, palm-cradled
 free-radical, went fading from a lamp next to her cot.)

'Well it seems to me you've just reduced all morality
to the same realm as the functioning of the autonomic nervous system.'

'In one way I have: but you ought to know by now
the body has a mind of its own. Many. And can it really be
that in the whole round of functions
and conditions you call "thinking," the will alone
should find and declare itself free? An uncaused cause,
the unmoved mover behind your actions? The place
of the will in your picture of cognition is curiously like
the place of the human in your picture of the world,
as if the part could summarily dismiss its interdependency
and assume control of the whole. Rumi gives the example
of a hand trembling from palsy,
the other trembling because your love slapped it away.
Both tremblings come from

God, yet you feel guilty about
the one.'

'Agenbite of outwit. Nevermind, just something I read.
Anyway, I don't think it's the notion of our own responsibility
that we cling to so much as *other people's*.
I can't imagine we could ever give up blame and judgment.
Another thing bothers me. The old story at least had some drama to it,
with our *choice* at center stage. But the way you tell it . . . what could creation
have *added* to the Infinite? What could the Infinite be lacking?'

'You've got it backwards. The elegance of Creation is in how it *subtracts*
from the Infinite. The miracle of the particular, the tesserae, the finite. Two
massively unequal celestial bodies are united, and crowned with totality's
corona: only at *this* place at *this* distance. The covenant of perspective. And
periodicity. To know the epic largesse, surely ye shall be changed. And tallying
the whole, to bear witness to the pageantry of part, the atlas of contour,
galleries of spectrum, to marvel at a sand dollar is to become, as the Sufis say,
the eyes and ears of God.'

'Even still, I gotta wonder, where's room for morality?'

'What if — I'm not saying, but what if — everything
unfolds as it has to? What if
everything you're doing is already right? I don't mean
perfect. We are all of us after all mediate beings in the
shadow realm of the imperfect. Right is a mediated word,
and rightly so — though so is perfect, though perfect would deny it.'

'My friend the physicist just might take issue with you on that one.
They've pretty much agreed now that God does indeed play with dice —
though he still gives a wide berth to the blackjack tables.
And the philosophers have agreed to continue disagreeing
on the subject of determinism, as well as on every other subject.'

'*If* determinism is, then your vaunted opposition of determinism
and freedom would itself be determined within this framework.
Moreover, *if* determinism is, then determinism *is* freedom.
Try and wrap your malingering mind around *that* one.
If you will the Way, the way is wide open. The path
is as unobstructed as a neutrino's.'

'Nutrin-O's? Sounds like a breakfast cereal.'

'They are so small all the universe appears to them like
empty space, which they freely traverse at the speed of light.
The point is that nothing is in the way of the Way, because
its way is what *must* be realized, without resistance.
External hindrances are an illusion.'

'Then whence my resistance to this conception?'

'You know the answer already: craving, aversion, ignorance.
The web of self-deception that is the basis of all suffering
existence: which is alright, that too is an unfolding part of your "being right,"
wrong-headed as it is. Just know that your resistance to determinism
is itself on one level a self-imposed limitation —
a willfulness turned against knowledge, against the knowledge that
knowledge itself is the locus of freedom, not the will.'

'But if you're right, that is, if I'm right, why isn't
that at all apparent to me? Why am I always worrying
about just that question?'

'Good question.'

'And so what can I do to stop worrying about it?'

'If I'm right, if everything unfolds as it has to,
then there's nothing more you can do to stop worrying.
So stop worrying!'

11
Of this number am I too now, a fugitive from heaven and a wanderer,
because I trusted in raging strife.
(Empedocles, Fr. 115)

How woundly I'm tight today,
swelled on Redstripe and sunstroke,
and the odd Tequila Mockingbird
(don't attempt this at home:
1 part tequila, or better still, mezcal,

to 4 parts cheap beer, bitters to taste,
approx. 1 jigger to a pitcher; garnish
with worm)
lugging an ungainly mind around,
a mind remanded to *gumbolimbo,*
that purgatorial okra-and-bird-lime slime
thickening your thinking here, metaphorically
speaking, and lugging around the avoirdupois
of my hard-bound Collected Spinoza, who says,
"All things excellent are as difficult as they are rare" — which
instantly makes it worth the weight.
Such idle musings beget — what?
Blandishments of abandon and
the Gordian Not: e.g.,
is not a sonata
is not in the scented batch
is not ingredient to the visible spectrum
is not in the pocket of vested interests
is not suitable for dinner conversation
is not a siphuncle
is neither syphilitic nor avuncular
is not Tartini is not the Devil's Trill
and so on and so forth
is not expressible in canonical notation
therefore is not quantified over
is not sord nor is it sloe
is not one of the five major foods groups
is not one of the Four Horsemen
is not equible
is not equine nor aquiline
is not worth quibbling over
is not Orpheus is not Orion
is not Dog Star
is not doorstop is not in any way functional
is not one of the above, is not yet hatched . . .
Catch my drift?
Truly, we just drift through these afternoons, hyaline
as an afterthought in the endless annals of ephemera. I'm reminded of a
buddhist concept, the *alayavijñana,*
or "storehouse-consciousness."
The eye of memory is lidless.

O.K. Here goes:
All men are mortal. True enough,
but who isn't these days? In all
the mulligatawny of human enterprise,
none is so tragic I think as logic,
oblivious as it is to the mortal irony
of it all. *Socrates is a mortal,*
one of the gang,
a laughing primate,
a higher vertebrate,
a reasoning princox,
i.e. the merely universal,
a.k.a. the un-unique.
Likewise, mutatis mutandis,
"papaya" is an "oblong to globose
edible yellow fruit."
Comprehensible, all too comprehensible.
And otiose o yes in a place like this
where wormlike reasoning appears
a blind vestigial process, and
dwindles thence to an appendix. Argal,
All men are Socrates, to one degree
or another I suppose.
Instead I propose how 'bout a lexicon
of affective definitions, according to
the mode sui generis. For example, "Pomegranate,"
how to put it, "articulates *in amore geometrico*
the geometry of delight," so far so good,
"so firmly is it fixed in a close-set, mildly
acid secrecy, a rounded sphere (sampling Empedocles here)
enjoying a circular solitude." In other words,
a typology of powers that freely calls upon the old affinities,
sympathies, signatures, *convenientia:*
don't tell me "godwit" is a wading bird
of the genus *Limosa.* I want to know
the secret hinted at by that sly upturned
bill of his. But what chance well you may ask has resemblance
when by an act of will (or is it more
a complicity of forgetting) we have
broken the hold of the old archetypes?
(What is owleffigy to the overmouse?)

Can't begin to say
I begin to say but can't,
tongue-tied
astride the rotting planks
hard by the mumbling waters of this
tidal river, the ever-contending
fresh and brine — haply
dumbstruck, mum as the ebb itself
"disembogued," a real word, meaning roughly,
gagged on ocean's stranglehold
(cf. Webster's *estuary*,
"an arm of the sea at the mouth
of a river"). And so it goes or doesn't
down there where the raw newcomers
will be making their tenderfooted way
back from the beaches, filing oblivious past
all the roadside barbecues
whose plucked chickens,
featherless bipeds,
await their turn at jerking.
Down where the several severed heads
of all the poets of all the rivers of Babble-on
are floated like coconuts to the sea,
whence like Orpheus they do make prophecy,
roughly speaking.

I confess, I'm tiring of our modern slack and slam.
O O O O that Shakespeherian Rap
It's so irreverent
so irrelevant.
I require a jacktar bard
who reeks of brine and Murphy's soap
and macassar oil hair pomade, whose
verse is so good it's tattooed
up and down arms like knotted hemp-line.
An old salt to show me the ropes —
'Dot yer tease and cross yer eyes.
Spit out yer gum and tie up
well yer tropes, lest you
trip over them.' To learn me
verbal knots no land-lubber

can figure, "bowline," "sheetbend,"
each syllable tied fast to the bight of the last.
To learn me fleet the metres and feet
and the three Ars of our profession —
reden, righten, and a rhythm tic.
Sapphics without affect.
Measures English or metrical
(but careful — not both. That's how
we lost that last Martian probe).
And spondees — prosody's couplet
gastropods. Let me be ever
drunken and spontaneous in rude
spondaics. Hexical lexical cant
to twine the masts in vine
and drive the bees crazy
from the hive . . .

How woundly am I tight today
swolled on redstroke and sunstripe,
mi belly a calabash,
my thumbs become marble busts —
Brahms and Wagner!
A distant radio, Mutabaruka
spinning Desmond Dekker
This is the face
of Fu Man Chu . . .
and the root man hobbles up
ram bamba loom ba
peddling his rasta nostrums
and afrodesiacs,
concoctions for every occasion —
Put-it-back
Pick-me-up
Irish Moss
Big Bamboo,
infusion and pressings of fruit and root —
Push tea
Mushroom tea
Sweetsop
Soursop
Papaya

Banana and
Beetroot.

'Well peg me spellbound to a cotton tree,
Ambassador Tom-tom of Taboo!'

'And a fine howdoyoudo to you.'

'Rastafarian is a barbarian in Barberland.'

'Reprehensible, all too reprehensible.'

'Bumbaclaat is the only word for it, mon.'

'Highly Selassie, I conjecture. Speaking for myself,
I'd rather be a pagan suckled in a creed outworn.
But as luck would have it I'm a Jew, and so I
share a certain skew modality with you: namely,
the Sense of Exile.'

'Ah, I've just the tea for your condition.
Take this brother, may it serve you well.
Perhaps you will come to understand
this harshest of truths:
Zion is Babylon, Babylon is Zion.
Also between these two is no difference whatever.'

Well color me zomboid! he was right, and now I've hit it —
the motherlode. Calling all Trapezoids.
Wire the Parallelepipeds.
Urgent parallelograms criss-cross the hemispheres:
Don't miss out on
the Prismoid Prismatoid Parade!
Visions hypnagogic dance in my head,
thought's illegible graffiti. Would I could tell all.
But what my tongue may lack in syllogism
it makes up for in ambidextrousness.
Prehensile, all too prehensile.
How fortunate to be captive israelite
smack-dab in the belly of abundance
rambam baloomba,

and to be gifted, moreover,
with opposable composers!

12

There is no use in crying over the sea
and there is no end to crying,
no end to the tide of lacrimae rerum.
Each wave unfolds, casts up its dead,
and lapses like spilt milk . . . .

Tonight, the first night
of an ancient universe,
I walked again beside the sea's refusal,
among the bits broken off from her effluxus,
the flakes of stunned energy
everywhere and always shaken off.
The sea you see is not only *dance* and *mastery.*
She is abeyance,
and this is her boneyard.
"An eddy of all manner of forms
is skimmed off from the whole" as Leucippus puts it.
Hell, it's all been said before, and better,
and better left unmentioned. Or merely noted,
as in the gnat *Nataraj* grained against the fading skyset,
corroded now to time's native hue,
that color most becoming of becoming, and pendant with
fixed stars and wanderers,
opulent as Croesus' purse — a king's ransom:
And Venus down in the violet band, brightest of all.
Imagine all the love in the universe
contracted to a single point (though really how could you?
so much of it effulging all around here)
and as you stare she binds you to her
with a blinding kiss acetylene
dripping sparks.

When I stooped to scribble this down
squinting in the last light, my glasses all salt-specked,
I noticed on my arm, no kidding, a winged ant
struggling with the wind

and with these gossamer fastenings, new cumbrances,
but managing, just, a hieratic dignity —
future queen of her kind!
Then trimming those ill-fitting things
she took to the sky, where suddenly
dozens then gazillions of her kin
virgin queens and holy drones frenzied in the nuptial ardor
began tracing graceful trajectories
about my head.
Why tonight must be the night
of the Queen Ant's Dance!
It is a stately alate
furious helical kind of a thing
a recombinant sort of thing,
really impossible to put into wording.
'Most grateful am I to your Puissancies,'
I gullivered, 'for allowing me to, um,
attend, the uh royal ball.'

Now the sky was all set about
with the Jewelled Net of Indra,
bits of Orion
glimpsed through drifting
palm tinsel,
and at the zenith the most
baroque turquoise cloudings,
a harem organdy
a turkish delight
in which the moon reclined
while I recline too, my head on a stone
dumbfoundering.
Here is revealed the order physics but conceives,
the spherical temple of Ultimate Equilibrium
whose girth is the earth
whose altar is water
whose stair is of air
whose spire is fire —
to put it peripatetically.
Peripatetic: "of or pertaining to a Greek
school of stand-up philosophers"
(Socrates: "Take my life — please.")

I say to any of you if any there be
who have given in to the sibilant summons of the undertow
or been unstrung by the symmetrical kiss
of a moon jelly,
and still made it grateful back to shore —
attend with the keener ear you have won
to that barbarous booming mantra
'boonoonus, boonooonusss':
for the roar of the sea is —
          laughter,
rolling, ironical, good-natured,
whitmaniacal laughter, spasming
sparagmosing in peals of guffaw.
The papaya, likewise is splitting its sides,
and the spider, the trickster Anansi,
of whom I spoke when I spoke
of the web and its hub
is in stitches — and now I too've got a bellyful in me,
flopping around like fish in a tidepool
waiting on the riptide . . . Jumpin' Jehosaphat!
That physicist was right on the money
in that dream of his — levity, that so leavens the head
it rises to the very firmament,
that so lightens the heart
a feather-weight drawn from the pinions of an ibis
is enough to tip the balance Anubis holds,
the jackal-headed judge and psychopomp
of the last mysteries of all.

And lo! are come on the
mighty surge —
mer-men from Mirth!
dressed in the blessèd dreadlocks of sea-tangle,
bearing rich gifts from the sunken coffers of sea-wit
(puns and conundrums),
ranting and belling up the very elixir sea chanteys
the sea chants to herself
of an evening on the island of Calypso . . .

I am beside myself with dismay.
Before, I had been, well, content to make a solitude
and call it a peace. But not no more.
What? A happy ending?

As to the rest, there is little left to tell.
Suffice it to say that before long
we three kings — me, myself and Dismay —
are instructed in the Most Secret and Scientific
Doctrine of Ebullience,
the ineluctable modality of the risible.